WILD ELEPHANTS IN CAPTIVITY

Dr. Jack Adams

Department of Psychology
California State University Dominguez Hills
Carson, California 90747

Center For The Study of Elephants
P.O. Box 4444
Carson, California 90749

Library of Congress Catalogue #81-69851
ISBN 0-942074-00-9

ACKNOWLEDGEMENTS

Without all the people who have shared their concern about elephants with me, this book could never have been written. I wish to thank the members of the "Smokey" Jones family for their help in gathering material for this book. I wish to thank Bob Kellogg of the Los Angeles Zoo for sharing with me his vast knowledge of elephants and people associated with them. I am very grateful for the friendly reception I received from all the elephant trainers whom I interviewed in the course of writing this book. I wish to express my appreciation for the encouragement I received from friends and colleagues by their frequent inquiries: "When will your book be finished?" I also want to thank the numerous people I have met who were associated with elephants in museums, zoos, circuses, cultural and government services in America, Europe and Southeast Asia who were willing to discuss elephant problems with me, and the courtesies they have extended to me during my visits. I want to express my gratitude to Norma Carlsen of the University Library for her assistance in obtaining inter-library loans of scarce and critical references. Grateful acknowledgement is made of the important photographic work of Cliff Brown of the University Photo Laboratory. Many thanks are also extended to Dr. Lyle Smith, for his critical reading of the manuscript. I wish also to express my appreciation for the patience and understanding my wife Beatrice has demonstrated during the course of writing this book. And finally, I wish to thank Margaret Garvin, June S. Turner, and Heather MacDonald Chronert for typing the manuscript.

PREFACE

I have had several reasons for writing this book. In the course of ten years of study of elephant behavior, I have observed many similarities between elephants and people. Believing in the evolution of human behavior from other animal forms, then we can see many antecedents and even similarities of human behavior in elephants. Therefore, I think it quite likely that a study of elephants may indeed be a course of insight and understanding of human behavior.

I would like to acknowledge the superb work and achievements of the great living circus elephant trainers.

I hope that in writing this book I have successfully presented under one cover, in easy to read form, much currently available knowledge about African and Asian elephants and how to care for and train them in captivity.

This book is directed to animal lovers, scientists, and to those who are in someway associated with elephants, such as zoo elephant keepers, circus elephant caretakers, and elephant owners and trainers who are interested in obtaining pertinent information about these majestic animals.

It is my hope that through the disemination of knowledge about elephants, their survival in captivity will be enhanced.

CONTENTS

CHAPTER 1

HISTORICAL INTRODUCTION

Numerous books have been written about the unique role of elephants in human mythology, religion, culture and economy throughout the history of mankind. Through these written accounts, benevolent attitudes have been developed towards animals so much larger and at times threatening to humans, not only in nature but also when under human care. Elephants have long been used as symbols of strength and integrity, and numerous literary accounts have described the ancient cults of the elephant and the existence of enormous marble elephant replicas in India, the gigantic stone elephants along the approaches to the Ming Tombs near Peking, China, and stone reliefs which are among the notable features of Angkor Thom, Cambodia. Many of the more recent references and monuments to elephants are less well known, and these bear mentioning as evidence of the perpetual human interest and affectionate relationship with elephants.

In the gardens of Bomarzo, Italy, there are numerous animal sculptures, among which is an enormous elephant. Commissioned by the nobleman Vicino Orsini in 1564, that elephant was fitted out for battle, with accoutrements similar to those on the elephants which accompanied the invading armies of Pyrrhus (280 B.C.), and of Hannibal (218 B.C.).

Fig. 1
An elephant sculpture in the Gardens of Bomarzo near Viterbo,
Italy. [Photo by Enit-Roma].

The granite elephant in the Piazza della Minerva, in Rome, Italy, is the work of Ercole Ferrata and it dates back to 1667. It is part of the base designed by the fountain designer Bernini, on which rests a sixth century B.C. Egyptian Obelisk. An inscription by Pope Alexander VII states that the elephant symbolizes the strong mind necessary for sustaining wisdom.

In classical antiquity and in medieval times, the elephant was considered a symbol of wisdom, purity and chastity—all the virtues which members of the chivalry were supposed to possess. To perpetuate interest in these virtues, The Order of the Elephant was instituted in Denmark in the middle of the 15th century, and it was proclaimed in 1693 by King Christian V. This honor is bestowed only on sovereigns and other royal persons, presidents, and particularly Danes and foreigners who are thereby accorded the epithet of Excellency.

The Kingdom of Thailand has an Order of the White Elephant, which was founded in 1861. There are several degrees of this Order ranging from medals given to ordinary citizens for outstanding service to the country to special medals of this honor to members of the royal family.

In the United States a huge elephant structure was erected as a public attraction. In 1882, an Elephant Hotel was built on the beach at South Atlantic City, New Jersey by James V. Lafferty, a real estate developer.

The body was 38 feet long and 80 feet in circumference, the legs 22 feet long and 20 feet in diameter, the head 26 feet long and 58 feet in circumference, the trunk 36 feet long, the tusks 22 feet long, the eyes 18 inches in diameter, the ears 17 feet long and 10 feet wide, and each weighing 2,000 pounds. The tail was 26 feet long, and the howdah or observation platform was 65 feet in elevation from the ground, 16 feet square and 20 feet high. Access to the interior was by way of a spiral stairway in the right hind leg; and the left leg provided an exit. The stairs contained 350 steps. Inside the Elephant Hotel there was an 18 x 18 foot

Fig. 2   The Elephant in Rome's Piazza della Minerva, bearing a 6th century Egyptian Obelisk on its back. [Photo by Enit-Roma].

MEDALS
OF THE MOST
EXALTED ORDER
OF THE
White Elephant
Kingdom of Thailand

Fig. 3 *Medals of the Most Exalted Order of the White Elephant in the Kingdom of Thailand.*

15

Fig. 4   The Elephant Hotel, an old landmark on the beach at Atlantic City, New Jersey.

reception room, and a dining room, kitchen, and four bedrooms. There were 22 windows in the entire building. In the erection of the giant elephant-like structure, over a million pieces of timber were used. There were 8,560 ribs or arches. Two hundred kegs of nails, and four tons of bolts and steel bars were used to frame the structure, and 12,000 square feet of metal to cover it.

The Elephant Hotel was considered unique and extraordinary in size and design during its time. It could be seen from a distance of five to eight miles, and it was a famous landmark and public attraction for many years. Steamships came in close to shore so that passengers could see the rare and unusual structure. Trolley cars were scheduled directly to the Elephant Hotel for tourists to view it at close range.

In 1887 the Elephant Hotel was sold to John and Sophie Gertzen who named the structure "Lucy." They claimed that it had been visited by such notables as President Woodrow Wilson, Henry Ford, the Asters, the Rockefellers, and many foreign dignitaries.

Later, the Gertzen family sold the site to a developer and offered Lucy free to the city if it could be moved. In 1970 the Elephant structure was moved a distance of two blocks to a city park. After the move, the then delapidated Lucy was restored with funds from federal and state historical grants. Now, about 25,000 people visit Lucy the Elephant every year, paying $1 admission. The name of the city is now known as Margate, New Jersey.

A profitable early American enterprise was the importation and exhibition of living zoological specimens. The possession of a tiger, camel or elephant was considered a sound investment. Hackaliah Bailey (of Barnum & Bailey, Greatest Show on Earth fame) was a partner in a menagerie business that owned at least one elephant named "Old Bet" on August 13, 1808. There apparently is no record of whether that elephant was of the African or Asian species, or of its age or sex. The traveling menageries, showing their "natural curiosities," were often joined by horse shows and other acts. These displays and demonstrations were known as "Educational Shows," and they were the origin of the American Circus.

The elephant "Old Bet" was reported as having been killed in Alfred, Maine on July 26, 1816, by a boy who was induced to test the claim that the hide was bullet-proof. He allegedly fired his gun into the elephant and the shot entered through the eye, killing the animal instantly.

In 1825, Hackaliah Bailey opened an Elephant Hotel in the Village of Somers in New York State. Considered one of the finest structures in the Colonial tradition of architecture, it played an important role in the life of the bustling community, serving as a regular stop for the stage coach lines between New York, Danbury and Boston. Many famous Americans stayed there as guests, including Aaron Burr and Washington Irving. Scenes for the movie "America," starring D. W. Griffith and Lionel Barrymore, were shot there. It now houses The Somers Historical Society.

In 1887, on the green in front of the Elephant Hotel, Hackaliah Bailey erected a memorial to his elephant. It was a wooden likeness, placed high on a granit shaft. The original memorial was destroyed by time, weather, and woodpeckers many years ago; but a replica of "Old Bet" on its original shaft still stands today in front of the Elephant Hotel.

Outside the Royal Museum of Central Africa in Brussels, Belgium, there is a huge concrete African elephant with three tribesmen on its back. It measures 25 feet from the ground to the tip of the elephant's raised trunk, and it is 18 feet long. Conceived by the artist-sculptor Alberic Collin, and created as an ornamental motif in front of the Pavillon de Congo Belge at the International Exhibition of Brussels in 1935, it was later placed on the museum grounds.

A cartoon of an elephant representing the Republican political party vote was conceived by the illustrator and caricaturist Thomas Nast. It first appeared in the November 7, 1874, issue of the Harper's Weekly Newspaper. The purpose of the elephant caricature was to impress on the public mind the absurdity and danger of two political and

Fig. 5
Replica of "Old Bet" on top of a granite shaft on the green in front of Hachaliah Bailey's Elephant Hotel in Somers, New York. [Photo Somers Historical Society].

Fig. 6   Elephant monument in front of the Royal Museum of Central Africa in Brussels, Belgium.

moral issues that were debated in America during the last century—the Democratic political party accusations of "Caesarism" against President Grant, and the concocted story printed in the New York Herald newspaper about dangerous animals that allegedly escaped from the Central Park Zoo and menaced the public. The symbol of the elephant was used because the animal was supposed to be clever and unwieldly, and although easily controlled until aroused, became unmanageable when frightened. Eventually, the elephant was accepted as a symbol of the Republican political party in America, and remains so today.

In 1915, Allan Hancock donated a 23-acre plot of land that included the La Brea Tar Pits to the County of Los Angeles in Southern California. The land was to be maintained as a scientific park. Tons of fossil bones have been excavated in the area. The George C. Page Museum was erected on the site in 1976 to display the numerous animal fossils that have been removed from the nearby tar pits.

Among the interesting and educational exhibits is a complete mastodon skeleton measuring six feet and three inches in height. There is also another mammoth skeleton measuring 10 feet and 8½ inches to the top of the shoulders, and 11 feet, 7 inches to the top of the skull. Using the dimensions of the reconstructed skeleton, a replica of a mastodon was constructed in fiberglass material and placed outside the museum. Also, using the dimensions obtained from the skeletons, a replica of a family group of mammoths has been erected. The display shows a large female mammoth submerged and trapped in the liquified tar pit. On the bank of the tar pit is a baby mammoth with a horrified look, and also a large mammoth, each extending its trunk toward the partially submerged female. This scene was supposed to depict what probably happened in the area thousands of years ago. The imperial mammoth was the largest of the great elephants that existed in North America before their extinction during the last Ice Age.

Fig. 7   Facsimile of the American Mastodon reconstructed from skeleton found in the La Brea Tar Pits in Los Angeles, Cal.

Fig. 8 Imperial Mammoth family reconstructed from skeletons found in the La Brea Tar Pits in Los Angeles, Cal.

Carl Jacobsen, son of the founder of the Carlsberg Brewery in Denmark, was a dedicated traveler, and wherever he visited he liked to draw copies of buildings, facades, etc., to take back with him to Carlsberg. While in Rome, he adored the elephant in Minerva Square, and in 1901 he asked his architect, Professor Dahlerup, to construct four elephants at the entrance to his brewery. The sculptor was H. P. Pederson-Dan, and the elephants were made of granite from the island of Bornholm. Today, the elephants at the brewery gate are a famous tourist attraction in Copenhagen, as is the Little Mermaid, which was also donated by Jacobsen.

In 1959, Carlsberg started brewing a very strong "Elephant Beer." Initially, the label on the bottle contained a picture of the elephants at the brewery gate. When observed from one side of the gate, only two elephants are seen. After appearing on the world market, the sale of this beer in Africa was in an unexpected slump. A study of public attitudes towards the beer revealed that the sight of two elephants represented bad luck in African mythology. Thereafter, the brewers added a third elephant to the picture on the label and the sales of the beer increased remarkably.

Carlsberg also brews an Elephant Malt Liquor for export, but the label on the bottle is not the same as the one described above. This label contains a humorous caricature of an elephant.

During my travels to several countries in Africa in 1971, 1973, and 1975, I was appalled at the plight of elephants in their diminishing natural habitats. I came to the conclusion that if elephants were to exist at all in the future, it would depend on our capability to maintain them in captivity. In my own research involvement with elephants, I have found a critical shortage of scientific information on elephants in captivity. Therefore, I have conducted some long term studies of elephant behavior in local zoos, and wild animal parks. Several publications have resulted from this research.

During October, 1977, I initiated action for the

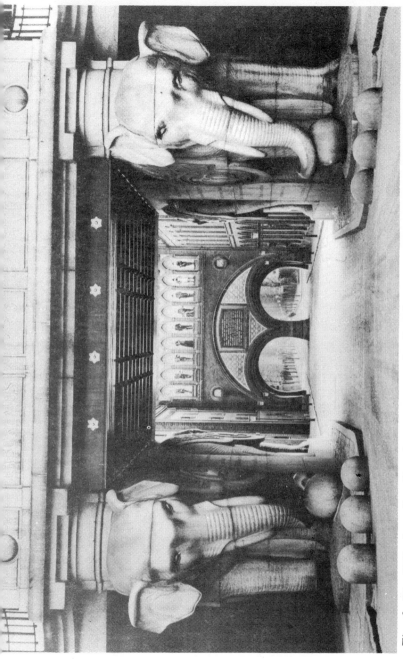

Fig. 9 The "Elephant Gate" at the entrance to the Carlsberg Brewery in Copenhagen, Denmark. [Photo by Burt Seeger].

25

Fig. 10   Carlsberg Brewery Elephant Beer label on bottles
intended for the African consumer.

Fig. 11   Carlsberg Malt Liquor label for export.

establishment of a "Center for the Study of Elephants" at the California State University Dominguez Hills, in Carson, California. The stated purposes of the "Center" are:

1. To solicit funds for research on elephant anatomy, physiology, diseases, nutrition, reproduction, and behavior, as well as on the care, management, and training of elephants.
2. To collect and computerize the storage and retrieval of scientific information on elephants.
3. To provide pertinent scientific information to interested persons, and to public and private institutions that are involved in elephant care, management and training. Presumably, such information is not now easily available to many.
4. To sponsor lectures, symposia and international conferences on various aspects of the biology or care of African and Asian elephants.
5. To research the need for Federal and State legislation regulating the importation, transportation, care management and training of elephants.
6. To maintain a census of African and Asian elephants in captivity.
7. To publish a journal for the dissemination of scientific information on elephants.

In conjunction with the "Center for the Study of Elephants," I have established an "Elephant Museum" at the University. The museum is exclusively dedicated to the exhibition of elephant fossils, skeletons, organs, teeth, fetuses, tusks and ivory carvings, stamps, coins, a graphic tribute to elephant trainers, photographs, paintings, etc. I have buried a dead adult Asian elephant on the campus and exhumed it several months later after the tissue decomposed to restore the skeleton for display in the museum. I have also buried and exhumed an adult African female elephant, and most recently a three year old baby African elephant, to display a "heterogeneous family" of elephant skeletons.

The museum provides scientists with physical elephant specimens for research. For the general public visitors the museum exhibits are reminders that unless we do something constructive about the preservation of live elephants, while they are still available, future generations of humans will only see the remains of what used to be African and Asian elephants, just as we now see fossils of mammoth and mastodon elephants.

A recent acquisition by the Museum was a life-size wooden elephant roll-top desk measuring 9 feet in length, 5 feet wide, 7 feet tall, and weighing nearly 1000 pounds. Christopher Schambacher, an art student at Central Washington University, carved the elephant from 600 board feet of laminated African shedua, a dark, walnut-like wood imported from Ghana. The drawers, writing surface and the elephant's tusks are made from birdseye maple wood. Everything from a chain saw to dental picks were used to sculpture the elephant desk. It took four years to complete. The elephant represents the sculptor's endeavor to create a unique but functional art object. It has been valued at $55,000.00.

Elephants have been destined to play an important role in mythology, religion, culture and economy because of their long relationship with human beings. No other animal has been accorded such an honorable recognition.

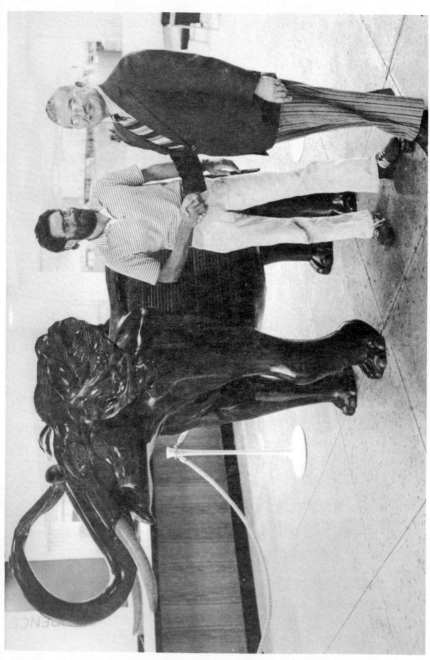

Fig. 12 The author and sculptor Chris Schambacher, alongside life-size wooden rool-top desk.

CHAPTER 2

WILD ELEPHANTS IN CAPTIVITY

Most of the elephants commonly seen in circuses and zoos today have been captured in their wild natural habitats in Asia or Africa at a relatively young age, and then trained to exist and perform in captivity.

The first elephant to arrive in America was a two-year-old female of the Asian species. Brought from India aboard a sailing vessel, the young animal arrived in New York on April 13, 1796. It was transported and exhibited in several New England States for many years and presumably died sometime after March, 1799, as no further record of its existence was available after that date.

The first African elephant in America probably arrived about 1824. It was a very young female and she was exhibited in a circus for many years.

The first elephant to be born in America was of the Asian species and it was purported to have occurred on March 10, 1880, at the winter quarters of the Cooper and Bailey Circus in Philadelphia. After living to an age of 25 years, it had to be destroyed when it became very dangerous. Subsequently, other Asian elephants were born to circus-owned elephants, but very few survived.

In August, 1916, the Liberty Park Zoo in Salt Lake City, Utah, acquired an elephant from the Sells-Floto Circus. The baby born to her in April 1918, is supposed to be the first elephant born in an American zoo. Unfortunately, the little elephant died a year later. The mother of this elephant was

31

obviously pregnant when she was sold to the zoo, as the gestation period for elephants is 22-24 months.

A more successful zoo elephant birth occurred on April 14, 1962, when "Packy" was born to the Asian female "Belle" and sired by "Thonglaw", at the Washington Park Zoo in Portland, Oregon. Subsequently, a series of Asian elephant births took place at the Portland Zoo. From a total of 19 born, 15 survived to over one year between 1962 and 1979.

The first birth of a baby African elephant in an American zoo took place at the Knoxsville Zoological Park, Knoxsville, Tennessee, on March 2, 1978.

Many large elephants of both the African and Asian species have been imported into America, and at least two of them have become famous for reasons other than their display in circus acts and menageries.

One of the two was an African male named "Jumbo." This elephant, while still quite young, was acquired by the Zoological Gardens of London, England, from the Jarden des Plantes, in Paris, France, on June 26, 1865. Jumbo was unusually docile, and for many years he was used for giving rides to children and for entertaining adults in the London Zoological Gardens. As he neared maturity, this formerly pleasant elephant became more and more unreliable and more and more aggressive. It was finally decided to put him up for sale. P. T. Barnum, the great American showman, purchased Jumbo and brought him to America in 1882. The considerable controversy over the sale of the elephant, involved the British news media, the Parliament, the Queen, and a public outcry urging a rescinding of the sale of Jumbo. When he was brought to America at the age of 21, Jumbo was a very popular attraction in the Barnum and Bailey Circus. He was estimated to be 11 feet tall and weighed 13,000 pounds—the largest elephant ever imported into the United States. Only two years later, on September 15, 1885, Jumbo was killed by a railroad engine at St. Thomas, Canada. The magnificent elephant's hide was preserved and donated to Tufts University in Boston, Massachusetts.

Unfortunately, it later burned up in a fire. The skeleton of Jumbo is still on display at the American Museum of Natural History in New York City. And his name has passed into the American vocabulary as the word *jumbo*, meaning extraordinary size.

The other famous American pachyderm was a female Indian elephant named "Jap," with a height of 8 feet and 1 inch, and a weight of 8,095 pounds. This elephant was subjected to extensive physiological measurements when she was not busy in circus engagements. In 1936, Francis G. Benedict, of the Carnegie Institute, published *"The Physiology of the Elephant,"* in which he reported carefully measured basal metabolic rate, respiration, heart rate, digestive processes and other bodily mechanisms of this one elephant. Benedict's data was the only authentic scientific information available on Asiatic elephants in captivity for many years, and it is still valid today.

As the imported circus elephants began to mature, they began to be more difficult to control safely. Many broke away from their circus menageries and caused considerable damage to physical structures as they continued on a devastating rampage until they were finally retrieved by their trainers and handlers. Some of the elephants were declared "killers" after having attacked a number of people. The circus elephant owners were becoming more reluctant to assume responsibility, and the more dangerous elephants were sold or donated to zoos. In the zoos the elephants were enclosed in relatively small but secure quarters and they were seldom if ever allowed to engage in their learned repertoires because of a lack of competent trainers and caretakers. Later, zoos began to purchase and import their own desired species of elephants.

George "Slim" Lewis, co-author of the book entitled: *"I Loved Rogues,"* spent a considerable time of his life working with elephants. He described the dangerous antics of several notorious elephants, among which were: "Tusko," "Black Diamond," and "Ziggy," during the 1930's. All of those elephants subsequently met untimely deaths because of their unmanageability.

Several accounts have since been reported of elephants that have been docile for many years and performed reliably in circus acts but suddenly turned on their trainers and killed them. Eloise Berchtold, a 52 years old female elephant handler, was trampled to death by a 6000-pound male Asian elephant named "Teak" before an audience of 250 spectators during a Gatini Circus performance near Montreal, Canada in 1978. The elephant had refused to allow circus workers to remove the woman's body from the ring. He would roar and lift his trunk if anyone approached. Eventually, it was killed by a police sharpshooter with four shots from a .458 calibre rifle while it stood over the woman's body. The elephant was declared to be in a condition of "musth," during which time its behavior was observed to be highly unpredictable.

H. Morgan Berry, came to fame in 1962, as the owner of the male Asian elephant "Thonglaw" and the female named "Belle" which produced the first successful series of births of Asian elephants in captivity at the Washington Park Zoo in Portland, Oregon. Unfortunately, Morgan's mangled body was found near one of his elephants named "Buddha," on June 27, 1979, on his animal farm in Woodland, Washington. The five-ton chained bull-elephant apparently spent several hours tossing and trampling the body before it was removed. It was not definitely ascertained whether Berry was killed by "Buddha" or suffered a heart attack and was later trampled by the animal he had trained since it was a calf.

I had a short visit with Morgan Berry just one day before his tragic death. He had appeared to be aggitated and depressed at the time, and very much unlike the usual jovial and friendly attitude I had noted on previous visits to his elephant farm. I have often wondered if this bizarre mental condition had anything to do with his subsequent death.

Most elephant handlers and trainers in zoos and circuses have suffered attacks by their elephants, both male and female and by both the Asian and African species. Some of these had been repeated episodes. Fortunately, most of

34

these incidents have not resulted in permanent disability to the caretakers. Just what precipitated the aggressive acts has never been determined. The Center for the Study of Elephants collects accounts of elephant attacks upon caretakers. The purpose is not to establish guilt or innocence, but to evaluate the information in hope of ascertaining specific patterns of elephant behavior which would be helpful in recognizing imminent attacks and thus preventing injury by avoiding the elephants under those conditions.

CHAPTER 3

ELEPHANTS IN RELIGION, CULTURE AND ECONOMY

Buddhism was a religious sect that originated in India about the 6th century B.C., and spread to Ceylon, Burma, Thailand, Cambodia, Viet Nam, Loas, China, Korea and Japan. The word Buddha means "the enlightened one." According to Buddhist mythology, the Buddha was born as the son of a king and was named Gotama Buddha. He was supposed to have entered the womb of Queen Maya in the form of a white elephant and later transformed into a human body. As an adult, Gotama Buddha gave up his royal existence, became a monk and wandered around the country preaching and teaching the precepts of personal conduct that would bring about calmness and tranquility of mind. Subsequently, the white elephant became the symbol of Buddhism, prestige, prosperity and political power. It was believed that possession of white elephants would bring power, success and prosperity to the owner and to the people of the country. Therefore, the aquisition of white elephants was one of the major causes of war among the early kingdoms of Southeast Asia.

Legend had it that when white elephants were found they became the property of the king, and he decreed that they be bathed, annointed with holy water, fed the most exotic foods, paraded among the populace, and housed in ornate pavillions on the palace grounds. One account stated that newly born white elephants suckled large breasted women who stood in long lines outside the elephant's pavillion to render the service. It was an eagerly sought after honor because the animal was considered an object of national pride and not exclusively the King's possession.

An English governess to the children of the King of Siam (now named Thailand,) Anna Leonowens, had written an account of her experiences and among which she described the role of the white elephant in the religion of that country. She claimed that according to Buddhist philosophy, each successive Buddha, in passing through a series of reincarnations, "must necessarily have occupied in turn the forms of white animals . . . particularly the swan, the stork, the white sparrow, the dove, the monkey, and the elephant." Therefore, "all white animals were held in reverence by the Siamese, because they were once superior human beings, and the white elephant in particular, is supposed to be animated by the spirit of some king or hero. Having once been a great man, he is thought to be familiar with the dangers that surround the great, and to know what is best and safest for those whose condition in all respects was once his own. He is hence supposed to avert national calamity, and bring prosperity and peace to a people."

There is no factual evidence that purely white, or albino, elephants have ever existed. However, today in Bangkok, Thailand, there are nine so-called white elephants in the pavillions on the palace grounds. Some of them are greyish in color, others have blotches of pinkish, or beige colored skin. The Veterinarian, Dr. Bamrung Watanarom, who made regular visits to examine the health of the beasts, stated that there were various characteristics that would be attributed to white elephants. These consist of five white points: white eyes, white palate, white toenails, white hair and white tail; and two white or pale pink points: including the color of the penis and the skin. Elephants with these characteristics are highly venerated in Thailand today.

The best known of the Hindu gods is Ganesh or Ganesha. According to Hindu religious mythology, Ganesh was supposed to have been the son of the goddess Parvati. He usually stood guard outside her door to insure her privacy.

Fig. 13 The Lord Buddha calming a runaway elephant

Fig. 14 The author and a Thai caretaker alongside one of nine "White Elephants" on the palace grounds in Bangkok, Thailand.

One day the god Shiva tried to enter but he was repulsed by Ganesh. Incensed by this affront, Shiva invoked the aid of Vishnu, the Preserver, who summoned a beautiful female spirit to preoccupy Ganesh's attention. Thereupon, one of Shiva's warriors decapitated Ganesh and Shiva entered the goddess Parvati's chambers. Upon learning of Ganesh's fate, the goddess became furious and obstreporous. In order to pacify her, Shiva promised to restore the head of Ganesh with that of the first animal he could find, which happened to be that of an elephant. Ganesh is usually depicted as a rolly-polly individual with a zest for frivolity, quick wit and superior intelligence.

A facsimile of the elephant-headed Ganesh is frequently seen on the walls near the entrance or on the doors of Hindu temples. This symbolizes his efficacy to remove obstacles that would hinder the faithful from veracious veneration of the Deity, and the search for spiritual inspiration. To many Indians of the Hindu religion, Ganesh is believed to be the god of intelligence, and therefore, the tutelary saint of students and teachers. While I was in Madras, India recently, an Indian colleague of mine carried a picture of Ganesh in his shirt pocket, in hope that this Deity would clear the obstacles towards his aspirations.

Elephants are deeply rooted in the traditions of the people in Southeast Asia even today. In India, there is the annual observance of the religious festival of Ramlila, which commemorates the slaying of the demon king of Lanka. Numerous elephants are painted and adorned in exquisitely colored brochades and paraded through the streets. Most Hindu temples own one or more elephants that are used in religious processions.

In Kandy, Sri Lanka, there is the annual observance of the pageant "Perahera," during which one of many caparisoned elephants carries the Sacred Tooth Relic of the Buddha through the streets in endless processions of elephants, monks, and converts.

Fig. 15 A wooden carving of the Hindu god Ganesh.

41

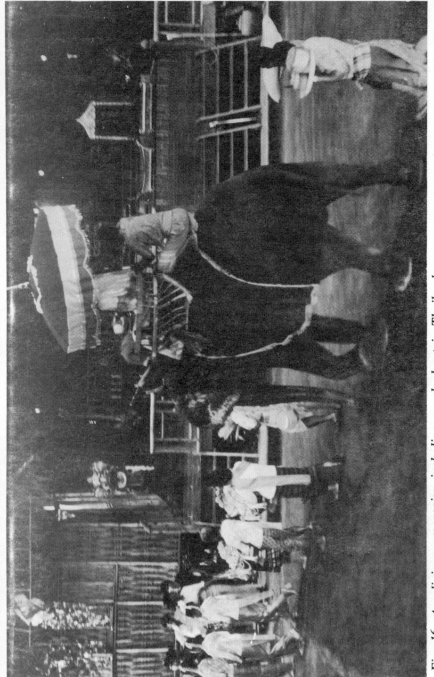

Fig. 16 A religious procession including an elephant in Thailand.

42

Elephants play a significant role in the cultural aspects of many countries of the world, especially in Southeast Asia. Private elephant ownership is a symbol of status, affluence and prestige, and the beasts are bequeted from one generation to another. Elephants are sometimes the only means of transportation during the heavy Asian monsoon rains, especially in inundated land areas. A few National Parks utilize elephants to convey tourists on animal observation safaris. Private entrepeneurs of elephants frequently establish elephant ride concessions in various tourist attractions. Tourists find this experience a rewarding accomplishment, and line up to take their turn in the "howdah" on the elephant's back. In America, elephant rides are usually available when the traveling circuses come to town.

A very popular cultural event involving elephants is the annual festival at Surin, Thailand. More than 200 elephants are assembled there from all over the country. There is a demonstration of elephant capturing procedures, simulated war battle, elephants engaged in a soccer game, and a tug-of-war in which one elephant overcomes the pulling strength of dozens of men.

Economically, elephants play an important role in the teak wood logging industry. In Thailand, Burma, India and Sri Lanka, hundreds of elephants have been trained to maneuver and drag huge logs out of the teak forests, to break up log jams in rivers, and to pick up and stack logs onto piles, either by themselves or in cooperation with another elephant. It takes five to seven years to train an elephant to work in the forests. Logging operations involving the use of elephants is a very tedious and slow process. Having observed the rapid and efficient mechanized logging operations in the Pacific Northwest area of the United States, I asked my Thai host, Dr. Trongwongsa, why his government did not speed up the logging operations by the use of bull-dozers, fork-lifts and other machinery. To this he replied that with the use of elephants there is no need to build roads, there is less

Fig. 17 Elephant carrying the sacred relic casket from the temple of the tooth to the Perahera in Kandy, Sri Lanka.

44

destruction of vegetation, there is no need to purchase high priced gasoline and oil fuel because the elephants derive their energy from the consumption of natural vegetation which is abundantly available in the forests, and one elephant provides the economic livelihood for two families—that of the elephant rider or mahout, and the elephant attendant on the ground—during the fifty years of the working elephant's life. However, with the declining numbers of wild elephants from which the working elephants are recruited, the extended periods of training, and the ever increasing demand for lumber, it is inevitable that most of the working elephants will be replaced by more efficient and economically feasible machinery.

CHAPTER 4

A TRIBUTE TO LIVING ELEPHANT TRAINERS AND HANDLERS

Elephant trainers are responsible for bringing the magnificent beasts to the attention of the general public. If it weren't for the elephant trainers, we would never be aware of the intelligence, gentleness, affection, docility, agility and strength of the ponderous pachyderms. Circus elephant trainers are responsible for giving the general public the impression that elephants are tame and responsive to every command. It is not generally known that it involved considerable risk to the trainers and that it took innumerable hours of hard work and dedication to develop a circus elephant act or to make the elephant obedient to commands. Through the results achieved by circus elephant trainers, elephants are considered to be lovable animals. It is no accident then that I have never met a person who disliked elephants.

Elephant Trainers are defined as persons who have "broken" a wild elephant. That is, they have taken a wild elephant that has been brought into captivity and trained it to become docile, to obey commands and to perform in an act in a circus or zoo presentation.

Elephant Handlers are persons who have trained and broken elephants to perform fantastic and incredible acts, but these people have never been actually involved in breaking a wild elephant. They are sometimes referred to as "bull hands." This is not to disparage the accomplishments of these elephant persons, but only to make clear the

46

distinction in the use of the terminology: elephant trainers, and elephant handlers.

Several books have been written which have described the exciting and adventurous exploits of many by-gone elephant trainers. This chapter is dedicated to the following *living* elephant trainers to let them know that their contributions, courage, ingenuity, hard work and dedication to the training of elephants in captivity is greatly appreciated.

Mac MacDonald is probably the oldest living elephant trainer. He was born on November 9, 1900, and he has spent 54 years in the business of elephant training. At 81 Mac is still active in training elephants. By general concensus of his colleagues, he is considered the "Dean" of living elephant trainers. He has trained approximately 45 elephants from a "green" condition into a circus act or obedient to commands. He is the originator of the one leg stand in elephant acts. His business motto is:"WE ORIGINATE — OTHERS IMITATE." Mac believes that elephants are the most intelligent among the four-legged animals. He bases that opinion on his observation that elephants learn readily from their experiences of what is expected of them, whereas other animals must be subjected to extended trials of rote repetition in order to learn certain trained behaviors. At the present time, Mac owns two Asian elephants, each seven years old. Mac's wife Peggy, frequently assists him in training elephants. The MacDonalds make their home in San Antonio, Texas.

Buckey Steele was born on February 16, 1936. His experience with elephants began with the Russell Brothers Circus. He has broken 16 elephants and he has worked countless others. He currently owns two Asian elephants named "Bukalee," a male aged 9 years, and "Zola," a female aged 14 years. He is currently active in circus elephant acts, and he frequently also engages in "cat" shows involving tigers, lions and leopards. Buckey feels very strongly that he has the human right to use elephants and other animals to make a living. Some of the problems Buckey has encountered in his circus elephant acts is the lack of secure areas for his elephants away from the public between

Fig. 18. Elephant with broken hind leg being treated. The leg...

acts. He has noted that the proximity of public strangers causes elephants to be perturbed. He believes that traveling circus elephants are healthier than zoo elephants because of the variety of hays and other foodstuffs they receive while the circus is on the road. Buckey is a very conscientious elephant trainer, totally dedicated to his elephants.

Barbara Tata owns three female Asian elephants: "Lulu," age 4 years; "Chang," age 7 years and "Wimpy," age 8 years. Barbara works her elephants alone in a two ring circus act combined with Buckey Steele. She is probably the only female elephant handler with a regular circus act involving elephants. She has also hand-raised five baby elephants. These accomplishments put her capabilities comparable with many men in the field of raising and handling elephants. Buckey and Barbara make their home in Seagoville, Texas.

Rex Williams was born on January 23, 1927, and he has worked with elephants for more than 35 years. He broke 31 elephants, and he has worked a number of others. Rex has trained many African elephants, a task more difficult than training Asian elephants. However, once trained, Rex believes that African elephants are more reliable than Asian elephants. He claims to be the originator of the elephant pyramid act in the United States. He spends a lot of time working with elephants, yet he readily admits that his elephant act is never perfect. He believes that captive elephants live longer in the United States than anywhere else in the world. Rex is currently associated with Circus Vargas in which he conducts an 11 elephant act. Rex's act is spectacular because he puts the elephants through their routines while he is mounted on a white horse.

His charming wife, Ava, is also a co-star in the elephant act in the middle ring. A petite 5'2" tall and 120 pounds, she is a very talented performer as she rides, climbs, and is twirled by an elephant during the show. The Williams' two children, Rene and Darlene, also participate in the elephant act.

Rex Williams owns two Asian elephants: "Gardner," male, age 11 years; and "Gyp," female, age 9 years. Rex named some of his elephants after famous elephant trainers.

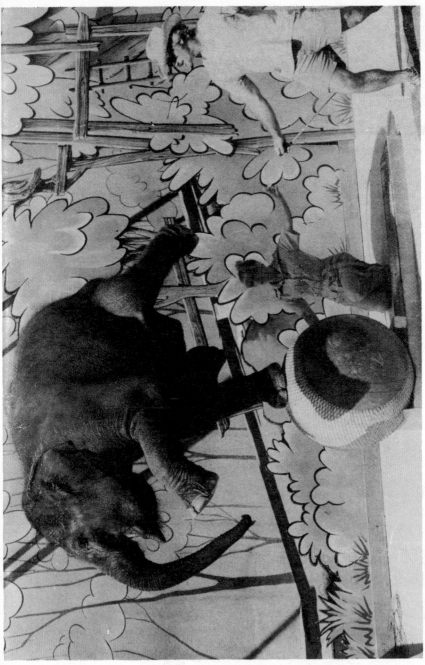

Fig. 19 A "Mac" Mac Donald trained elephant. It rolls a large solid metal ball into a well and then does a awoloo stand Handlors aro Francino and Phil Schakt

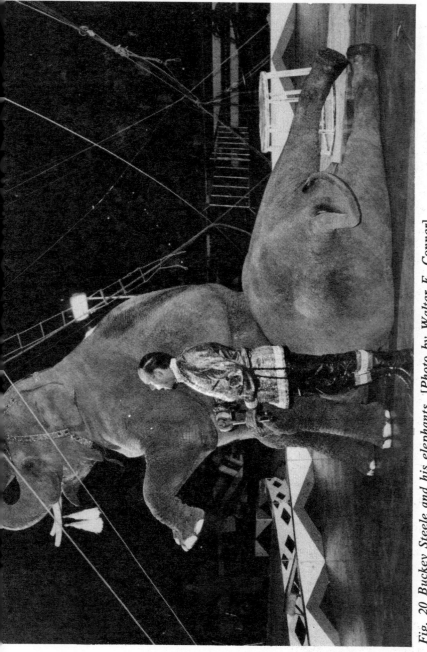

Fig. 20 Buckey Steele and his elephants. [Photo by Walter E. Conner].

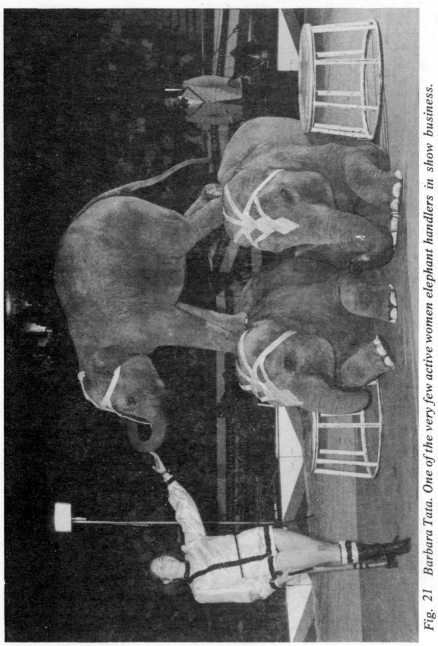

*Fig. 21 Barbara Tata. One of the very few active women elephant handlers in show business.
(Photo by Walter E. Conner)*

The Rex Williams' make their home in Myakka City, Florida.

William "Buckles" Woodcock was born and raised in the circus elephant training business. He has learned elephant training from his famous father Colonel William Woodcock, Sr. In his middle forties, Buckles was the superintendant of the 22 elephants of the Blue Unit of the Ringling Brothers Barnum and Bailey Circus. In addition to his regular work of presenting his elephant act, Buckles is a circus historian and he keeps a census of elephants in captivity as a hobby.

Buckles Woodcock and his gorgeous wife, Barbara, have enjoyed their association with the "Greatest Show on Earth." Their elephant act is spectacular because they have combined a beauty and the beast. Barbara is a beautiful, attractive and talented show person who is a conspicuous contrast to the massive elephants. She climbs over them, walks under them, and finally permits herself to be either held in the trunk and whirled by a giant pachyderm or carried by her knee in the mouth of a hugh Asian elephant. One is so fascinated by Barbara's performance that it is easy to forget that the intricate and precise movements of the massive elephants are actually the obedient responses to the commands of Buckles Woodcock, their trainer. Two Woodcock children are also involved in the elephant act. He believes that training elephants is a very dangerous business because of their huge size and great strength. The Woodcocks make their home in Ruskin, Florida, when they are not on the road with the circus.

Gunter Gebel-Williams, his "cats," and elephants were the leading acts of Germany's famous Circus Williams for many years. Gunter came to America in 1969, and at the age of 44 years, he is the star of the "Red Unit" of the Ringling Brothers Barnum and Bailey Circus. The circus management has insured his life for two million dollars. He started training elephants in 1956. During his current three-ring, 22 elephant act, he claims he directs the elephants through their routines only by voice command. One of his incredible acts is a magnificent number in which a large elephant

Fig. 22 Rex Williams and his wife Ava. [Photo courtesy Vargas Circus]

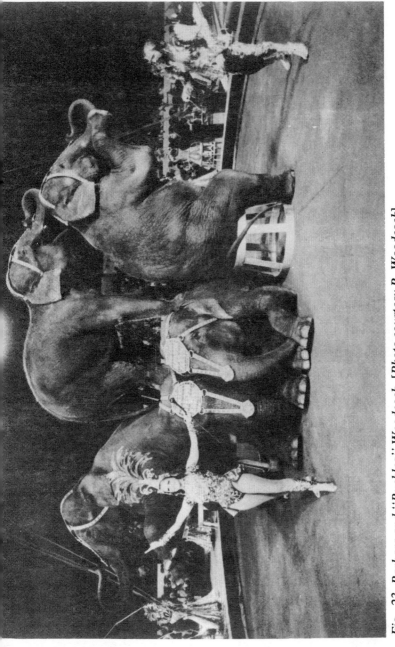

Fig. 23 Barbara and "Buckles" Woodcock. [Photo courtesy B. Woodcock].

lumbers up to one end of a teeter-board, steps on it, and hurtles Gunter from the opposite end into a backward sommersault and up onto another large elephant's back. In other acts he has mixed elephants, horses and tigers, which are supposed to be traditionally incompatible animals.

Gunter believes that training elephants to perform tricks enhances their brain power and makes them happier and healthier animals. Gunter, his strikingly beautiful wife, Sigrid, and their two children reside in Venice, Florida, when they are not on the road with "The Greatest Show on Earth."

Robert "Smokey" Jones was born in Hoxie, Arkansas, on January 3, 1927. He was nicknamed "Smokey" because of his sooty face which he acquired from riding freight trains. Smokey's first exposure to elephants was at the age of 16 years when he was hired as a "Bull-hand" on the Dailey Bros. Circus in 1946. The superintendant of the menagerie was Louis Reed who took a liking to the young runaway kid who was making a strong impression on the old man by his hard work, devotion and dependability. It wasn't long until Smokey was given more and more responsibility around the menagerie and he was measuring up to the tasks. Reed soon began to restrict Smokey's work to elephants only and he was determined to make the kid his protege by giving him personal instructions and hints on handling and training elephants. The new relationship made Smokey work even harder in trying to please Reed who was like a father to Smokey. He had a feeling that Reed was proud of his work with the elephants, although Reed never actually praised him. Smokey remembers the event that gave him some inkling that Reed considered him a responsible "bull-hand." It was when Reed instructed Smokey to get on top of Rosie, a huge Asian Elephant, and ordered him to take her to water. It was a very scary and exciting experience, and Smokey couldn't believe he was so high up as he strattled the elephant's neck with his legs and commanded her to proceed to the water trough.

There were 25 elephants with the Dailey Bros. Circus, and

Smokey obtained considerable experience in all aspects of elephant care, management and training under Reed's tutelage. When Reed left the Dailey Bros. Circus, Smokey was ready to try things out on his own. He joined up with the Al G. Kelly Miller Circus where he helped Colonel Bill Woodcock break elephants in winter quarters and then he went on the road with the show. He next took a job working a male Asian elephant named Charlie with the Circo Union in Mexico. It was during his work with this circus that he learned to write his name upside down and backwards in order to autograph the pictures put in front of him by admiring fans. He then worked with the Campa Bros. Circus for a short time. He rejoined his old mentor, Louis Reed, at the Ringling Bros. Barnum and Bailey Circus in 1952. This period was probably the highlight of Smokey's career as an elephant trainer. His work in training elephants was so outstanding that it came to the attention of one of the owners of the circus, John North. Louis Reed told North how efficient and experienced Smokey had become, so North asked Smokey to take over the training of the 51 elephants of the Ringling Bros. Barnum and Bailey Circus.

Smokey was an outstanding boss elephant man. While the Ringling show was on the road, the elephants frequently had to be moved from the railroad siding to the area of the circus location. Smokey would lead the long procession of 51 elephants in ranks of two while he rode on a white horse and wore a spotlessly clean white shirt. This was the largest number of elephants ever taken from coast to coast across America.

Smokey became extremely proficient in tying fancy rope knots and in making and using long bull-whips made from rope and leather. He found the use of the bull-whip much more efficient in controlling elephants than the bullhook.

He knew all of his 51 elephants by name and he could recite their names like a littany. During this time, Smokey allegedly had the reputation of being the roughest, toughest and most ornery elephant man in the business. An extensive chapter was written about Smokey by Bill Ballantine in *Wild Tigers and Tame Fleas* which was published in 1958,

Fig. 24
*Gunter Gebel-Williams. Photo by permission of Ringling Bros.
Barnum & Bailey Circus*

and in another article entitled: Taming the Seven-Ton Killers: Brutes of the Big Top, in *True* magazine in 1960.

During the next two years the Ringling Bros. Barnum and Bailey Circus elephant shows were being converted from outstanding elephant acts to spectacular productions surrounded by colorfully clad dancers, clowns, and acrobats. Spats were placed on the elephant feet and hats on their heads. Labor and economic problems continued to plague the circus management. Reduction in spending on maintenance of the elephants and cuts in staffing were being constantly urged upon Smokey. Not willing to compromise the health and training of his elephants, Smokey finally terminated his association with the Greatest Show on Earth.

After 1955, Smokey drifted from one circus to another. He settled down for a while in Texas during the early 1960's. In Fort Worth, he conducted a school for elephant care at the zoo. He worked elephants in Six Flags Over Texas. And, he worked three elephants on Kilroy's Ranch in Wallis, Texas. One of the elephants rode in a cadillac convertible. His work with elephants soon had him on the move again. He worked for Murray Hill in Burlington, Wisconsin putting an act together with some "punk" elephants named the "Mighty-Mites." With an elephant named Tonzo, he later participated in a stage version of "Around the World in Eighty Days" in Atlanta, Georgia. In 1967, Smokey went to Bangkok, Thailand, to buy three elephants for Sid Kellner. Later that year he was in Martinez, California, winter quarters of James Bros. Circus, putting another act together and then going on the road with that show. In 1968, Smokey worked Judy the water-skiing elephant at Marine World in Redwood City, California. Later that year, he "broke" five small elephants for Morgan Berry in Woodland, Washington. In 1969, Smokey was with the Hamid-Morton Circus winter quarters in Trenton, New Jersey, training elephants and then going on the road with the show working five elephants. For the next three years Smokey was involved in numerous short term engagements involving elephant acts for various elephant owners in Canada, the

U.S. and Mexico. In 1972, Smokey bought and received a baby elephant from Thailand and named her Tika. From that date until 1980 he was engaged in training Tika and taking her on various road shows. The task involved his whole family including his wife, Beverly, stepdaughter, Kari, stepsons, Jay, Keith, Ken and son, Jerry.

During his 32-year career of elephant training, Robert Smokey Jones had trained 56 elephants by himself and 26 elephants with Louis Reed. Smokey is undoubtedly the most knowledgeable and experienced elephant trainer in the business. He is highly regarded in that exclusive fraternity of elephant trainers in which only a few persons can honestly claim membership. The elephant world is indeed fortunate that Smokey has agreed to reveal his method of training elephants in the basic routines which will be described in a later chapter in this book.

Robert Smokey Jones is only physically 5'10" in height and 200 lbs. in weight. He has a short neck, a barrel chest, and powerful arms. He wears his hair cut short. He looks like a defensive guard of a championship football team. He is extremely strong, as an elephant trainer should be.

Although Smokey has no formal advanced education, he is extraordinarily knowledgeable about a lot of things. He is an acute observer of not only elephants, but also the behavior of his family and associates. He regards this characteristic as extremely important in elephant training. He is very punctual and it irks him if people are not on time. Smokey is an honest man, and he can't tolerate people with phony claims to cover up their mediocrity, and he doesn't hesitate to speak out against incongruities and inconsistencies. He is highly meticulous and a perfectionist in his work and he expects his associates to be likewise. In preparing for training an elephant, he gives each detail considerable thought and planning. He is obsessive about details, and compulsive about the placement of ropes, stakes, and other necessary equipment. He believes that a well-thought-out project will facilitate the training of elephants and minimize the probability of injury to personnel and the animals. There is no question that Smokey is in charge when it comes to elephant training. He gives the naive observer the impression that he is rough and tough and sometimes even what appears to be brutal. However, Dr. William Higgins, a veterinarian who has worked many years with Smokey on the Ringling Bros. Barnum and Bailey Circus, described Smokey's deportment as firm and in command of each situation. Smokey obviously knows from many years of experience what tragic episodes can result if the slightest contingencies are not anticipated when working around potentially dangerous elephants. All of Smokey's elephants soon learn that he is dominant over all of them and that they will be rewarded for acceptable behavior and negatively reinforced if they respond in an unacceptable manner. Smokey has never abused or crippled an elephant, and he is intolerant of anyone who mistreats them in any way either physically or by negligence. Although Smokey has received some minor injuries from elephants, his realistic philosophy has kept him out of the hospital and his name out of the obituary column during his 32 years in working with elephants.

One of Smokey's trademarks is his cleanliness with elephants and equipment. Elephants under his care are never allowed to start the day in a dirty condition. If it was too cold to wash them in the morning, he would just scrub the stains and wash their eyes out. Later when the weather warmed up, the elephants would get a bath and the stains would wash off easily. Smokey has often been accused of running-up the water bill by washing elephants and the barn too frequently.

On every show that Smokey and his family did with their elephant, Tika, everything that went with them was scrubbed—Tika, the truck and trailer, and all the props whether they would be used or not. One of Smokey's common sayings was: "We never went anywhere when everything wasn't clean and in class-A shape. I'm pretty proud of that myself."

Smokey has always been very selective about the jobs he

accepted. He never takes a job that doesn't pay top dollar. He would work free for charity, but never cut-rate. He set very high standards for himself, especially when he was showing Tika, their elephant, and he stuck to them.

In relating her impressions of Smokey, his stepdaughter, Kari, gave the following intimate opinion after observing him at training elephants:

If you just walked up and saw him in the process of "Breaking" elephants, you would think that he hated them. If you understood what was going on, you would see all the special care and understanding he has for them. Smokey's method of training elephants is quite unique. First of all, he really loves elephants! He enjoys making them as comfortable as they can possibly be. He loves just being in the barn and watching them eat. It may sound a little bit corny, but when the elephants are most contented, Smokey, is most contented. He believes in taking care of their mental as well as their physical well being. When the elephants are in training, they are usually confused and upset. So Smokey sets aside certain times of the day just for their relaxation, such as early in the morning when they finish their first walk. He turns them loose and lets them kind of clear their heads. The elephants Smokey works on are the most important thing in the world to him. Every day is planned around them. From morning until night the elephants are first in his mind. He watches and controls everything including feeding, exercise, bowel movements, play and training. Smokey seems to understand a lot more about elephants than he realizes. When there is a problem, he seems to know what to do even though he couldn't explain why himself. I suppose it comes from years of paying attention to elephants, but it looks like magic to me. I've seen Smokey take a sick elephant, look it over and find something nobody else saw or thought about. He would change the diet, exercise it, keep a close eye on it and pretty soon the elephant was normal again. He doesn't believe very much in using injections and medicine. As long as we owned Tika for six years, she was never given a shot and she was never sick. All he used was deworming medicine and antiseptics. I guess you could say that Smokey thinks the natural way is the best. Now I've made him sound like a magician or a healer. Of course, that isn't true. Smokey gets upset with me for saying things like that. He says that I'm just dreaming and that it's just common sense and doing what should have been done in the first place. But I'll repeat, it looks like magic to me. You could more easily believe what I have said if you could see him walk into a barn containing strange elephants. Everything changes. I could swear the elephants know who he is or they seem to know that someone of authority has appeared in their midst. They usually make that low rumbling noise and come to attention if he goes near them. I've never seen an elephant, even one with a bad reputation that knocks people around, ever take a swing at Smokey. Somehow they know better.

Robert Smokey Jones was strongly opposed to the government intervention into the regulation of elephant importation, care and management. He considers it a grossly emotional over-reaction, not necessary and illogical. He cites an analogy that all the motorists' drivers licenses are not suspended because one driver has an accident. Therefore, all elephant owners should not be subjected to bureaucratic regulations because a few people have neglected their responsibilities. He contends that most elephant owners, caretakers and trainers are responsible people who usually provide adequate and humane treatment of their animals. He does admit, however, that a few thoughtless cases of neglect should have been subjected to disciplinary action. Smokey foresees a gradual decline in elephants in captivity when elephant owners find government restrictions intolerable. This is a gloomy outlook for the future of elephants as their numbers are also rapidly diminishing in their wild natural habitats. If elephants are to be allowed to exist at all, their survival will depend on their care in captivity. We don't know enough about elephants to restrict their existence in zoos only. Private elephant owners and circus elephant trainers are also capable of contributing a considerable amount of knowledge toward our understanding of these magnificent beasts because they are in contact with their elephants much more frequently than zoo elephant caretakers.

After two previously unsuccessful marriages, Smokey Jones married Beverly Hough in 1965. His bride already had a family of a girl and three boys by a previous marriage. He wasn't quite sure he was capable of facing up to the task of raising four little children. However, he assumed his responsibility with determination. He immediately legally adopted the children and began to raise them in his own image. He and Beverly subsequently had one additional child, a boy named Jerry.

Many people who meet the Jones children are impressed by their unusually good conduct, and Smokey's usual retort is that he trained the children just like he trained elephants. Perhaps one of the children's own accounts of their training may reveal what it was like:

> We kids were quite young. We hadn't much real discipline though I don't think we were too bad. When Smokey and Mom were married, things began to change and our formal training began. He didn't like the way we talked, ate, played or anything else. He thought we were sissys so he built us a treehouse and made us play in it. Every meal was like a lesson.

"Eat everything on your plate, don't spill anything, and don't fool around," were the usual commands. We had to do dishes, sweep the floor and clean up after ourselves. Smokey was adamant about putting the lid back on the toothpaste tube, and you better not squeeze the tube in the middle. During this training period we all got plenty of yelling at and spankings. He would drill us a lot, like in the Army I suppose. We called everyone "Sir" or "Ma'm." When he called us, we had to respond immediately with "Sir?" and run toward him. If we didn't answer loud enough or come fast enough, we would have to go back to where we were and do it over again. We would repeat this until he was satisfied that we got it right. He demanded the utmost respect and attention.

One would expect the children to resent such apparently tyrannical conditions, but here is what one of them had to say about their upbringing after reaching adulthood:

I understand now that Smokey was trying very hard to make us the best we could be. At the present time it just seemed like he hated us. However, when I see my brothers compared to others their age, I am proud of how they turned out. Smokey hadn't had any previous experience with children so he treated us just like elephants, although I believe the elephants had it easier. When they did a certain trick correctly, the pressure was off. With us kids, he never let up. I suppose I'm grateful for my training, but I wouldn't want to go through it again. Smokey took five snotty-nosed little kids and turned us into what he thought we should be. You have to take your hat off to him. That may have been one of his toughest accomplishments. I will be eternally grateful to him for taking me off that farm in Wallis, Texas, and turning me into what I am. I feel I'm a much better person because of Smokey's guidance.

Most people would predict that the children would leave home as soon as they became of age, but four of the children are of legal age now and they are all still living at home.

Smokey and his family moved from one state to another as his work demanded. The children were unable to attend regular schools so they were enrolled in a correspondence school. Four of the children completed a high school education with outstanding grades. The fifth child now is enrolled in American Correspondence School, even though Smokey does not travel for extensive periods of time anymore.

In 1972, Smokey imported a female baby Asian elephant from Thailand. It was named Tika. The entire Jones family participated in cooking the hitherto secret formula (now revealed in this book for the first time,) and they all took turns administering the four-hour feeding schedule of the baby elephant. It was also a family project when Tika was being trained as a performing elephant. At six years of age, Tika had the most extensive repertoire of any performing elephant in the history of elephants in captivity. Among others things, she could do a head stand, hind leg stand, lay down, sit up, walk on a rolling barrel, sit at a table, ring a bell, play a harmonica, and drink a beverage from a bottle. Most recently, Tika was taken on a tour of several states for the Bell Telephone Company. In addition to her regular acts, Tika was trained for a promotional stunt in which a telephone would ring, Tika would take the receiver off the hook with her trunk, utter a sound, and "hand" the receiver to Kari who was her handler on this tour. Tika had performed on television, in circuses, schools, hospitals, and shopping malls. She could ride escalators, elevators and climb stairways. She was trained not to urinate or defecate while on stage during a performance. Bob Kellogg of the Los Angeles Zoo payed tribute to Smokey by stating that Tika's repertoire was the epitome of elephant training and that only elephant trainers could appreciate that.

Tika was never left unattended while on the road or at home. During the night-time hours, two of the Jones boys

Fig. 25 Robert "Smokey" Jones [on white horse] elephant "boss-man" at Ringling Bros. Barnum & Bailey Circus during the 1950's.

would be with Tika, and only one would attend her during the day. Tika was a pampered elephant, well fed, watered, and frequently bathed and scrubbed. She never had a sick day. Her quarters were always immaculate.

Smokey spent a lot of time passing on his extensive knowledge of elephants to his daughter Kari and his sons.

Smokey is quite a family man today. They all do many things as a group. They go for auto rides, attend the horse races, and go to swap-meets, and circuses. Smokey seldom goes anywhere without at least one member of the family with him. Smokey and his family make their home in Rialto, California.

There are a number of outstanding living elephant handlers who probably have either assisted in training "green" elephants or who have trained "broken" elephants. Some of them may have even "broken" a few elephants on their own. These men have done commendable work. Some of those who should be recognized are: Morgan Berry, who owned several elephants in Woodland, Washington; Don "Oakie" Carr, who is with the Carsen and Barnes Circus; Val De Leon, Knowland Park Zoo, Oakland, California, who helped Smokey Jones train elephants during his vacation periods from the zoo; Ben De Wayne, who has "Hollywood Elephants;" Tommy Donoho, who has a newly trained African elephant in Las Vegas; Bobby Gibbs, with the Carsen Barnes Circus #2 Unit; Axel Dotier, at Circus World in Orlando, Florida; Gary Jacobs, who works with Buckles Woodcock in Ringling Bros. Barnum and Bailey Circus; Gary Johnson, with Jungle Wonder Circus; Scott Riddle, at the Los Angeles Zoo; Wally Ross, at Moorpark College Institute of Wild and Exotic Animal Studies; Franz Tisch, with the San Diego Wild Animal Park; Al Vidbel, who has an independent elephant act; and George "Slim" Lewis, now retired.

Four women have already been mentioned as outstanding elephant persons and a fifth name is also worthy of mention. She is Kari Jones, who at the age of 21 is probably the youngest female elephant handler in the business. She is the

Fig. 26 "Smokey" Jones lecturing his daughter Kari and sons Keith, Ken, Jay and Jerry on the finer points of elephant training, with Gary Johnson looking on.

daughter of Smokey Jones. Kari who actually grew up with Tika, was actively involved with her father in the training of that elephant. A charming show girl, Kari directed Tika through her trained routines when Tika was involved in circus acts and show business.

The general public should be eternally gratfull to all these outstanding circus and zoo elephant trainers and handlers for bringing the magnificent elephants to our attention in so many interesting and entertaining ways. Allen and Kelly, in their book, *Fun By The Ton*, asserted that elephant persons didn't do it for fame, but tons of fun.

Fig. 27 Kari Jones and "Tika". Kari is probably the youngest female eleph handler in the business.

CHAPTER 5

THE SIMILARITY OF ELEPHANTS AND HUMANS

Did all human behavior suddenly appear in homo sapiens or can much of the same kinds of behaviors be observed in other animals? A study of elephants reveals that indeed there are many similarities between the behavior of elephants and humans.

Elephants have a life span of approximately 70 years, which is similar to the average life span of humans. Elephants suffer the same diseases as humans, including athereosclerosis and pneumonia. Female elephants are among the few mammals who have mammary glands in the anterior part of the body as in human females. Elephants live in closeknit groups or families. Elephant mothers take good care of their babies and even foster the young of other mothers that may be unable to do so due to sickness or death. Baby elephants are allowed to suckle from any lactating female in the herd. Elephants help a sick or fallen comrade by attempting to lift one from a falled position, and they physically support and assist an injured or sick animal of their kind. Some elephants of a herd stand guard while others lie down to sleep, or drink water. Elephants form a protective circle in times of uncertain disturbance, with rear ends together and heads facing outward, their young in the hub of the circle. This is a reminder of the defense strategy in old pioneer wagon trains when they were attacked by Indians during the American western expansion. Although elephants do not actually bury their dead, they have been known to cover carcasses with earth and brush, and to carry away tusks and bones of dead comrades. Elephants have lived in a variety of climates. They have been seen at the snow levels of mountains and of course in the heat of the areas of their natural habitat near the equator. Elephants eat a variety of foods including green and dried foliage, fruits, nuts, and roots, and, if the opportunity presents itself, they will invade agricultural areas and eat the vegetables grown by farmers. Elephants have a good memory. They seem to know when to return to areas where certain foods are in season, or where a water hole is located, and to remember the tricks they have been taught in captivity. Elephants are inquisitive and exploratory in ways that remind us of human behavior. Elephants manipulate objects if available. They fondle and caress each other, which is also a human characteristic. Elephants communicate by sound (at least seven different vocalizations have been identified) and by the position of the head and trunk, which could be analogous to human speech and gestures. Elephant herds are led by the largest and strongest female, whose sagacity and experience assures the survival of the herd. In human families the father is usually the financial provider, but the mother usually decides the day-to-day activities of the family group. Elephant skin is tender and subject to sunburn, so elephants apply mud-packs and they dust their skin with sand to prevent irritations. Could women have learned from elephants to beautify their skins with cosmetics? Elephant legs are similar to human extremities. Elephants have wrists and ankles, and they fold their legs like humans when lying down, unlike many other animals. Tool use is not an exclusively human endeavor; elephants use their trunks to hold objects like tree branches or vegetation to scratch themselves. Elephants bathe their bodies like humans. Unlike humans, elephants avoid the heat of the day, tho this is certainly more adaptive than the behavior of some humans in the tropics. Elephants feign sickness or disability just like human hypochondriacs.

Elephants are also subject to disorders which appear to

resemble human mental disorders. They may attack their caretakers without apparent provocation after years of docility—"manic aggression." Elephants also indulge in alcoholism while in their natural habitats, when they imbibe fermented jungle plums. The resulting behavior mimics the human staggering and loud vocalizations. In some parts of Asia, drug-addicted elephant caretakers have shared opium with their animal, making them drug dependent.

Additional similarities to humans include ability to modify their habitat by digging in the ground in search of water and minerals; uprooting trees and vegetation destruction; naked skin; deferred sexual maturity; and long developmental stages.

Thus there is ample avidence that elephants have many characteristics and behaviors that are similar to human beings.

CHAPTER 6

MUSTH AND THE TEMPORAL GLAND

Musth was a term used to describe a phenomenon observed in male Asian elephants at maturity (maximally between the ages of 21 and 30 years) and it was characterized by periodic bouts of excitement, disobedience and aggressiveness. The duration of this condition ranged from several days to several months. It was more likely to occur in healthy, well-fed male elephants than among those that were poorly fed and emaciated. This condition was supposed to occur in feral as well as captive elephants. Musth was also correlated with maximum seasonal rainfall.

The more specific behavioral manifestations that have been observed to occur just before, or during the musth condition included: erratic feeding habits, tendency to disobey commands from the regular caretakers, and attempts to mate with available females. If the female elephants did not make themselves readily available to the male in musth, he usually became aggressive and frequently inflicted injury on them. In cases where sexually receptive females were not available, the male in musth had frequent erections of the penis and repeatedly struck the tumescent organ against his abdomen. This behavior was interpreted as a form of masturbation.

Because of their extraordinary behavioral changes while in a state of musth, the male elephants were considered dangerous not only to their caretakers but to other elephants as well. It was the customary procedure to securely restrain an afflicted male elephant by rear and foreleg chains and to hand feed him on a reduced ration.

In addition to the marked behavioral changes while the male Asian was in a state of musth, there was penile erection for extended periods of time with concomitant dribbling of urine. There was also a profuse discharge from the bilateral temporal glands. It was the general consensus among elephant caretakers that musth was a phenomenon common only to adult male Asian elephants.

However, several conflicting reports have appeared in the literature indicating that female Asian elephants in captivity have also occasionally demonstrated recalcitrant behavior and simultaneous temporal gland discharge, and this deportment was also characterized as related to a female elephant musth condition. It was also noted that male Asian elephants in musth did not regularly mate with available females, and that some males copulated with receptive females when the males showed no signs of musth. In addition, some males came into musth repeatedly and not in relation to any periodicity or seasonal rainfall. Observations were reported in which wild Asian elephants were described rubbing their temporal glands against tree trunks and other vegetation following their mud baths. This gave rise to the notion that the secretion from the temporal gland was odorous and was used in marking the environment. These paradoxical accounts left the condition of musth in a state of confusion and misunderstanding.

Explanations as to what caused the phenomenon of musth were speculative and controversial. One writer suggested that musth was symptomatic of a liver disorder because there allegedly was a depigmentation of the skin. Another explanation was that the sexual activity produced a musth condition.

This muddled state of affairs prompted some scientists to investigate the physiological correlates of the musth condition. They selected the temporal gland as the subject of their study. In 1963 a study was conducted in Ceylon (now named Sri Lanka) on the temporal glands that were excised from a 2-3 month old male Asian elephant. Anatomical and histological analysis revealed that the temporal glands were comprised of tubular alveoli aggregated in lobules, similar to mammillary or milk gland tissue of other animals. Another study, done in collaboration with scientists from the same country and from England, in which 11 adult elephants were used, demonstrated that when Asian male elephants were in full musth, at ages 26-30, the testosterone levels in the peripheral blood plasma was extremely high. These scientists concluded that musth in elephants was comparable to the rutting behavior of some seasonally breeding-mammals.

Recently, the aggressive behavior of male Asian elephants in musth was explained as comparable to the androgen-induced aggression found in rodents, deer and domestic bulls. It was, therefore, hypothesized that if male Asian elephants could be castrated, then the production of testicular androgens would be eliminated and the associated aggression would also be eliminated and it would no longer pose a serious problem in management of male Asian elephants in captivity. To castrate a male elephant would necessitate major surgery because the testicles are undescended and located high up near the kidneys inside the peritoneal cavity. The first time such an operation was performed the elephant died. However, a successful castration was performed on a circus elephant by a veterinarian at the University of California, Davis. Total aggression has not been eliminated from the repertoire of behavior of this elephant. He still has periodic bouts of aggressive behavior and he occasionally takes swipes at his caretakers. However, his handlers agree that the castrated male Asian elephant is more manageable now than he was before the surgery. Another male Asian elephant in a circus recently attacked and seriously injured his handler without apparent provocation. There were signs of secretion from the temporal glands during the attack. The owner decided to have the elephant castrated before his aggressiveness resulted in a fatality of one of his handlers. The following photograph was taken while the castration surgery was in

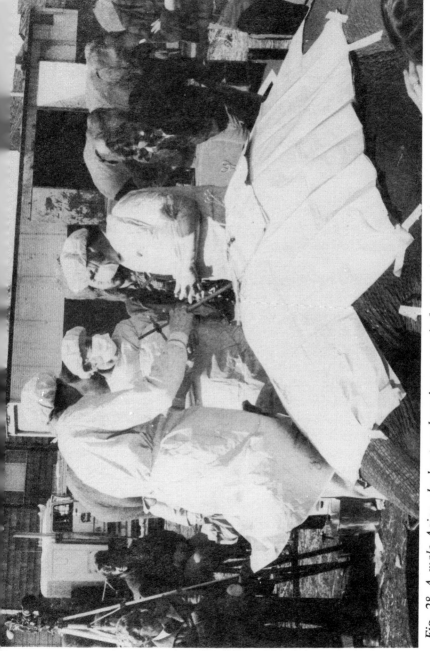

Fig. 28 A male Asian elephant undergoing a surgical castration procedure.

progress. Only one testicle was removed during a four hour surgical procedure. The elephant recovered satisfactorily and resumed his usual role in the circus elephant act two weeks later. Three months later the same elephant was again subjected to the surgical removal of the other testicle. About an hour into the surgery, the elephant suffered cardiac arrest and expired. As far as is known, only three elephant castrations have been attempted, and two of the elephants have died either during the surgery or shortly thereafter. A mortality of two out of three cases suggests that castration, at present, is not a very successful procedure. Death from castration is a tragic loss considering the good health of the elephant, the economic investment, and the many hours involved in training the animal.

Adult male Asian elephants are magnificent animals, especially when they have large tusks. However, the tusks of most male elephants in captivity are routinely cut off because the animal inevitably uses them as weapons to impale a victim during a period of aggressiveness while in a state of musth. If castration would reduce or eliminate the tendency toward aggressive behavior, it might be accepted as a routine surgical procedure for male Asian elephants in captivity. The elephant's tusks could be allowed to grow to their natural size, management of the elephants would no longer be a serious problem, and the public would enjoy viewing these gigantic creatures as they existed in their natural habitats. There is of course the opposite consideration: castration procedures obviously render the male elephant sterile. At present there are very few known breeding Asian bull elephants in captivity. The existence of Asian elephants in their natural habitats is already seriously impaired. If the propagation of Asian elephants is to be perpetuated, it will become necessary for them to reproduce in captivity. Therefore, if breeding elephants in captivity is to be successful, it will be necessary to have available male elephants that are capable of impregnatiing receptive females in estrus. Artificial insemination of female elephants has not been successful. This is the current state of our understanding of musth and the temporal gland in male Asian elephants.

Contrary to what one might expect, musth has never been reported in male African elephants. However, during the latter part of the last century and during the early part of the present one, elephant hunters in Africa described a mysterious secretion on both sides of the head of the male elephants that were shot for their large ivory tusks. Much folklore and mythology was associated with this secretion. African natives used it as a good luck charm any piece of wood found imbedded in the opening on the side of the head from which the secretion was expelled.

Systematic scientific investigation as early as 1916 revealed that African elephants, of both sexes, possessed temporal glands in the same area of the head as the Asian male species. Some anatomists described these structures as modified and complicated sweat glands. Other writers classified them as scent glands. More recent histological studies have identified the temporal glands in African elephants as apocrine cutaneous glands consisting of lobules of compound tubular alveoli. From a morphological standpoint, the temporal glands in both the African and Asian elephants are similar.

With the advent of the cropping operations in the National Parks of Africa in the 1960's to control elephant populations, it became possible for scientists to study the anatomy and physiology of African elephants. Often, entire elephant herds were wiped out, and scientists were able to examine the corpses and to study many parts of the elephant body including the temporal glands. Considerable data was obtained and correlated with sexes and ages of the dead elephants. From these and other studies the following facts were established: The temporal glands are active in both sexes and in all ages of elephants. (The author observed the temporal glands secreting in calves as young as one year of age.); the glands increased in size and weight with the age of the elephants; neither the size nor the function of the temporal glands were in any way related to reproductive

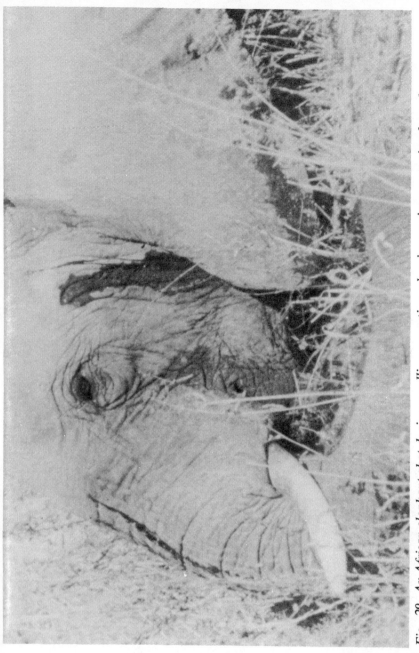

Fig. 29 *An African elephant shot during a culling operation, showing copious secretion from the temporal gland on the side of the head appearing as a dark vertical streak. Photo from an*

activity. Pieces of wood, bark and sand were frequently found embedded in the external duct of the temporal glands; testicular testosterone levels were extremely variable and not correlated with temporal gland activity; that the exudate was strongly odoriferous; that there was significantly greater activity of the temporal glands during the dry season; that during mating the temporal glands did not secrete in either the male or female elephants; and that the temporal glands secreted profusely when the elephants were frightened or excited.

On the basis of such evidence, and a considerable amount of her own data, a female Loxodontologist, Sylvia Sikes, speculated that the temporal glands in African elephants functioned as scent glands—providing information about territoriality, herd-identity, and sexual receptivity.

I and my colleagues were among the first to analyze the chemical composition of the exudate from the temporal glands of wild African elephants. In our 1973 research, it was discovered that the major chemical component of the temporal gland secretion was cholesterol. This was reported at the Annual Meeting of the Animal Behavior Society held at the University of Illinois, Champaign-Urbana, on May 26, 1974.

Since cholesterol production is associated, among other things, with stress and excitement in human beings, it was necessary to ascertain if the activity of the temporal glands was related to stress and excitement experienced by elephants. This author, therefore, went to Kruger National Park in South Africa, and Wankie National Park in Rhodesia in 1975 to conduct experiments on live wild elephants to test a hypothesis regarding the relationship between stress-excitement and temporal gland activity. Six adult male elephants were immobilized with etorphine hydrochloride (M-99) which was administered by a dart gun. As soon as an elephant dropped from the effects of the tranquilizing drug, 5 cc. of sterile epinephrine was periodically injected into an ear vein. In five of the six elephants used in this study, it was noted that at approximately 30 seconds after the injection of

Fig. 30 The author injecting epinephrine into an ear vein of an anesthetized wild African elephant to test the function of the temporal gland.

the epinephrine, at least one temporal gland began to secrete. Each elephant received three injections. At the conclusion of the experiment, an antidote was injected into an ear vein and each elephant regained consciousness without apparent ill effects, then ran off into the bush. The results were interpreted as confirmatory evidence that the temporal glands respond to circulating adrenalin and that the glands are related to the sympathetic nervous system which prepares the animal for fight or flight or for lesser degrees of stress and excitement.

The next experiment was designed to determine if the temporal glands could be made to secrete under stressful behavioral conditions. Small elephant herds consisting of 5-6 elephants were chased through the bush with a helicopter for 30 minutes. One elephant in each group was then immobilized by etorphine hydrochloride injected by a dart fired with a dart gun from the helicopter. When the darted elephant dropped from the effects of the drug, and the other elephants had dispersed, the helicopter pilot landed his craft near the immobilized elephant and this author examined the temporal glands of the recumbent animal. In each group of elephants, the darted one showed secretion from the temporal glands after being harassed by the low-flying helicopter. Based on the results of this behavioral experiment, it was concluded that the Arfican elephants' temporal glands secreted under conditions of stress and/or excitement.

It was also observed on other occasions that the temporal glands of elephants secreted profusely during culling operations when a low-flying helicopter forced a herd of elephants to move on the ground toward the direction of armed park rangers who shot all of the elephants, except the very young calves, at close range. The deafening flapping noise of the helicopter rotor blades, the unusually strong wind of the prop wash, the crackling sounds of exploding rifle cartriges, and the furious trumpeting and other sounds of the charging and dying elephants certainly may be considered an exciting and stressful experience for the elephants.

A more recent study was conducted by this author in collaboration with colleagues (Dr. Chris Foote and Alex Garcia III) in the Chemistry Department of the University of California, Los Angeles. By the use of mass spectrometry and gas chromatography, it has been found that the secretion obtained from the temporal glands of African elephants shot during a culling operation, contained more than 40 different compounds. Among the chemical components that have been tentatively identified are: phenol, p-cresol and m-cresol, indole, benzoic acid, and isomers of ethyl phenol, propyl phenol, ethylene diphenol (dihydroxy bibenzyl,) farnesene and farnesol. Analysis of the chemical constituents of the secretion from the temporal glands of the African elephant is continuing, and work has been initiated toward the chemical analysis of the secretion from the temporal glands of Asian elephants during musth.

Based on these chemical findings some preliminary behavioral studies had been conducted with one male and five female African elephants at Lion Country Safari, a Wild Animal Park in Laguna Hills, California. A variety of solutions, including pyridine carboxaldehyde, a synthetic mixture of cresols, natural temporal gland secretion, and water, were randomly presented to each elephant individually. The elephants spent more time sniffing the natural temporal gland secretion than any of the other solutions. There were no other obvious or significant changes in the behavior of the elephants. Therefore, whether or not the temporal gland secretion of the African elephant is a type of mammalian pheromone could not be ascertained from this behavioral study.

In another behavioral study on other African elephants in captivity, certain animals appeared to be secreting profusely from their temporal glands during periods of stress and excitement, but the sight or odor of glandular secretions did not appear to affect the behavior of the other elephants in the enclosure. It was considered doubtful that the secretion had any communicatory function.

On the basis of the numerous observations, studies, and experiments that have been described here, it can be concluded that the temporal glands of the African and Asian species of elephants are similar in structure but apparently different in function. In the male Asian elephant the temporal glands are related to a condition of musth and sexual activity, whereas in the African elephants of both sexes the temporal glands are related to stress and excitement but elicit no response from nearby animals. Much research will have to undertaken in order to resolve some of the inconsistencies and to advance our understanding of the role and function of the temporal glands in both the African and Asian species of elephants.

CHAPTER 7

THE INTELLIGENCE OF ELEPHANTS

One of the most frequently asked questions about elephants is: "How intelligent are elephants?" Before this question can be answered it is necessary to make some preliminary explanatory comments. Traditionally, intelligence was considered an exclusively human trait, and the behavior of animals was thought to be directed by instincts. Intelligence was defined as a capacity for reasoning, understanding, making use of abstract concepts, and effectively using past experiences in adjusting to new situations. Contemporary psychologists maintain that there are three types of intelligence instead of a single trait: verbal, mechanical or nonverbal, and social. The amount of intelligence in humans was measured by standardized intelligence tests composed of progressively complex test items. The score thus obtained was presumed to be a measure of the individual's intelligence. A score of 90 to 110 was considered to indicate normal intelligence. Human beings were expected to adapt and master their environment through their ability to exercise the faculty of intelligence.

Charles Darwin, a biologist to whom credit is given for a theory of evolution, maintained that human beings evolved from lower forms of animals. In discussing this relationship to lower animals, Darwin suggested that human intellectual powers were different only in degree and not in kind from certain vertebrate animals. This idea that human and animal behavior were in many ways similar gave rise to

Comparative Psychology, the study of animal behavior.

Intelligence in animals came to mean the ability to cope with the environment through learning. Animal behaviorists maintained that most animals exhibit a certain degree of intelligent behavior from complex reasoning to simple learned responses. The testing of animal intelligence was a major problem since the tests used in quantifying human intelligence could not be applied to animals. It was obvious that animals do not have the facility of language or the human capacity for manipulating objects. And it became apparent that tests would have to be devised that would be valid and reliable methods of assessing animal intelligence.

The first system used to quantify animal intelligence was the anecdotal method. The intelligence level of various animals was measured in terms of human capacities required to perform similar acts. Uncritical use of this method tended to over-estimate the intelligence of animals and it led to the application of the Law of Parsimony to animal behavior: "In no case may we interpret an action as the outcome of the exercise of a higher psychical faculty, if it can be interpreted as the outcome of the exercise of one which stands lower in the psychological scale." This canon prompted scientists to reexamine the previous claims of animal intelligence and to analyze complex animal behavior into simpler elements. Consequently, they found that many of the anecdotal descriptions of animal intelligence could be interpreted in terms of instinctive predispositions or conditioned responses to cues of which the experimenter was unaware.

One method for comparing intelligence among animals was based on the relationship of brain weight to body weight. It was hypothesized that quantitive changes in the nervous system would correlate with a series of qualitative changes in behavioral capacity. It was also thought that increased brain complexity would result in increased multiple determination of action, the ability to collect more diversified information, and thus more adaptive behavior. The ratio of brain weight to body weight for humans is 1,140 grams of brain to 70,000 grams of body weight, and 5,000 grams of brain weight to 2,500,000 grams of body weight for elephants. For each pound of body weight in humans there is 7.5 cc of brain volume, and for each pound of body weight in the elephant there is 1½ cc of brain volume. On such a scale, the ratio between body weight and brain weight places the elephant below the non-human primates and nearer the dog and the horse. Some physiologists maintain that the obsolute size of the brain itself, that is, the number of neurons in the brain that are capable of accepting, analyzing, storing and retrieving information is a better index of intelligence. From this point of view it is contended that the bigger the brain, the greater the brain effectiveness, and this relationship seems to be a general rule as we compare the members of the animal kingdom. The elephant has the largest brain of all land mammals, and probably the greatest capacity to learn.

Today, animal intelligence testing methods attempt to measure such factors as ability to learn, to solve new problems, or to create unique solutions to familiar problems. Because of their massive size, elephants have not been routinely studied in the laboratory. However, one systematic study was conducted on the learning capacity of a five-year-old Indian elephant in a zoo in Munster, Germany, more than twenty years ago. The elephant's task was to discriminate among various visual patterns such as a cross vs. a circle, and various other combinations of symbols. On the first attempt at the discrimination learning test, the elephant required more than 300 trials, over several days, to learn the correct symbol. However, once the elephant learned the correct pattern, she selected only the correct and rewarding symbol and none of the others. The elephant learned to discriminate more rapidly on subsequent tests, and by the fourth pair she was able to select the correct symbol after only 10 trials. The elephant could also keep simultaneously in memory the correct symbol of 20 stimulus pairs. She was also able to select the correct symbol out of four patterns that were presented simultaneously. In a test of ability to transpose learning or to form an abstract concept, the correct symbols were altered, a black cross to an X position, or extension of the arms of the symbols, etc. Regardless of the extent of the modification of the correct symbols, the elephant still recognized the figure as a positive or correct sign. It was concluded that the elephant was indeed capable of concept formation. The elephant also comprehended the concept of numbers. She successfully distinguished three from four circular dots regardless of their arrangement. The elephant's memory was also tested, since there is an old adage that an elephant never forgets. This elephant had retained the meaning of 24 different visual patterns for a period of approximately one year. Another study was conducted on elephants at the Portland Zoo in which an adult female Asian elephant was tested on a light-dark discrimination problem, with an eight-year period between testing. The elephant took only six minutes to reach criterion and she made only two errors. These two studies confirm that elephants have at the least, remarkable memories. This ability to learn is probably attributed to the elephant's exceptionally large brain. Although the dinosaurs had considerably larger bodies than the elephants, they had proportionately smaller brain to body ratios, and this was probably a contributing factor to their failure to adapt to their environment and thus their ultimate extinction. Therefore, using human and animal criteria of intelligence, the elephant has scored high on such tests as learning, reasoning and memory, as tested in experimental situations.

Another criterion of intelligence which is difficult to test in a laboratory situation is adaptation to the environment. Confirmatory evidence in support of this ability is plentiful in the natural habitats of elephants. Under natural conditions elephants were migratory animals, and they followed the seasonal rains and thus assured themselves of sufficient green vegetation for their diets. They also remembered the location of water holes. The routes they selected as their pathways through the forests and savannahs were terrains that were the most direct and offered the least resistance. Highway engineers came to realize that elephants did indeed select the best routes and these elephant pathways subsequently were converted to public roadways.

Elephants have continued to survive under extremely adverse conditions, being constantly forced into areas that they would not normally inhabit, as the demand for land for agricultural, industrial and housing needs expands in developing countries where elephants naturally exist. In times of drought or shortage of adequate food, elephants frequently abandon their regular sanctuaries and invade the nearby farmlands in search of food, with consequent loss and destruction of crops. A recent National Geographic Society documentary film: "Last Stand in Eden," clearly depicted this problem in the African country of Kenya. This sort of thing has occurred many times in other countries where elephants exist.

Human intelligence was supposed to be superior to animal intelligence because humans were tools users, whereas animals were thought to be incapable of this behavior. However, this criterion of intelligence has been found to be invalid because a number of animals have been observed to use tools in a variety of meaningful ways. Egyptian geese break eggs by dropping a stone on the shell; sea otters open clams by smashing them on a rock held on the chest while floating on their back in the water; chimpanzees select the appropriate diameter of a twig from a bush or tree, strip it of its leaves, insert in into termite holes, and extract termites which they eat. Elephants also use tools in a meaningful way. They hold pieces of wood or a bunch of hay in their trunk and rub parts of their body. The author recently observed several Asian circus elephants independently pick up flattened beverage cans with the trunk and scratch various parts of their body, such as under the chin, around the mouth, between the legs, and on the feet after they were soaked with water by their trainer. So tool using is no longer an exclusively human attribute, and if that behavior is a mark of high intelligence, the elephants have demonstrated it effectively.

Anecdotal accounts of elephant intelligence are legion

among elephant handlers, caretakers and trainers. Although these accounts are sometimes subject to exaggeration, they are worth mentioning in support of the extraordinary intelligence observed by persons who work around these animals daily.

A circus elephant was chained near a hay and grain barn. This elephant was capable of removing the steel bolt in the latch that kept the door to the barn locked. The elephant manipulated the bolt until he worked it out of the latch, dropped it to the ground, pulled open the door to the barn with its trunk, and fed on the grain and hay. This episode occurred on at least three different occasions. Each time that the bolt was removed and the barn door opened by the elephant, a trainer would scold the elephant and close the barn door by replacing the bolt into the latch. On about the fourth time this episode occurred, the trainer could not find the steel bolt that was usually dropped near the door by the elephant. A lady observer standing nearby informed the trainer that the elephant had been extending its trunk high up to a window ledge that was located above the door. The Trainer obtained a ladder, climbed up to the window ledge, and found the steel bolt that was placed there by the elephant. Was the elephant trying to hide the steel bolt so the door to the barn could not be locked by the trainer? The trainer was sure of it, and he claimed that this was the most intelligent behavior he had ever seen an elephant perform in his more than 35 years of experience with elephants.

Another account describes an elephant that was chained near a wall of a building, and the elephant was attempting to grasp a cigarette butt with its trunk, but the butt was out of the elephant's reach. After several unsuccessful attempts to reach the object, the elephant expelled a brisk breath of air from the trunk at the wall forcing the cigarette butt to roll nearer to the elephant where it was reached easily and consumed.

There are numerous accounts of elephant intelligence in relation to their work in lumber camps in Sri Lanka, India and other Asian countries. Elephants seem to understand the concept of balance and symmetry in loading and stacking timber logs.

Elephants have no natural enemies in their natural habitats. In a physical confrontation with human beings, elephants usually emerged victorious, but with the invention of firearms by mankind, elephants have learned that their only enemy is man. Therefore, elephants have tended to avoid contact with man, except when motivated by hunger or thirst. Also, after elephants have been trained in captivity through negative reinforcement administered by a trainer with his bull-hook, elephants tend to respond appropriately to verbal commands and a simple placement of the bull-hook on their body. So elephants have learned that discretion is the better part of valor. This certainly would be interpreted as intelligent behavior.

The comparison of elephants and humans in another chapter of this book supports the contention of the high intelligence of elephants. Thus, from experimental and anecdotal evidence there is sufficient data to support the notion that the intelligence of elephants would be ranked below the non-human primates but above the dog and the horse in the phylogenetic scale of animals. Are elephants intelligent? Indeed they are!

CHAPTER 8

ELEPHANT PERSONS

Anyone who contemplates being directly associated with elephants in captivity should first seriously consider the awesome responsibilities, commitment and confinement involved in such an undertaking. Physical property damage, serious personal injury and even death may result if proper orientation is not obtained. A trial period of experience around elephants would soon determine if one measures up to the requirements. Charisma is more beneficial than a "macho" attitude. However, for various reasons practical experience may not always be possible. So this chapter will attempt to delineate as vividly as possible what life is like around elephants, and what kinds of personal attributes contribute to making a great elephant person.

An elephant person may be any human being who owns, handles, takes care of, manages or trains elephants. This definition could also include anyone who loves, admires, or enjoys reading about or being around elephants. So, in the first place we have elephant persons who are in some manner directly involved with elephants; and on the other hand we have people who are indirectly involved with elephants. This book deals primarily with the first category of elephant persons. However, the second category of elephant persons need not stop reading here, because reading this book will give them greater insight and understanding of elephants and the persons associated with them.

Physically, an elephant person should be strong. There is a lot of hard work around elephants that involves lifting, climbing, carrying, pulling and throwing. Sometimes, one may engage the assistance of others, but more often one is left on one's own recognizance, so strong muscles are a definite asset. Height and weight are of lesser importance.

Mentally, the elephant person should be of sound mind. That means that the person should be at least average in intelligence, of strong character, honest, and have a realistic self-concept.

Emotion is an affective or feeling state in which love, joy, sorrow, fear, hate, etc. are experienced. Therefore, an elephant person must be stable emotionally because uncontrolled emotion can effect one's manner of thinking, feeling and acting, sometimes with devastating consequences. In times of emergency around elephants, keeping cool is essential so that the most logical options are considered and acted upon.

Love, understanding and respect for elephants, are also highly desirable. As stated in a previous chapter, I have never met a person who disliked elephants, but to be associated with elephants, one should have a certain fondness or affection for them.

In their natural habitats, elephants have managed to successfully adapt to their environment. However, in captivity, it is the responsibility of those to whom elephants are entrusted that these magnificent beasts are provided with the basic needs for their survival. Therefore, responsibility is a very important human attribute when working around elephants in any capacity. Responsibility also involves protecting the public around elephants, and also protecting the elephants from the public.

Commitment and confinement to the vicinity of the elephants appeared to be so obvious among great elephant trainers and handlers. These attributes were especially apparent among circus elephant trainers and handlers. This author was always cordially accepted by circus elephant trainers, and they were willing to be interviewed within the confines of the elephant area, but they refused to be lured away from the locality of their elephants for any prolonged length of time. Their whereabouts were always known. There seems to be a strong sense of dedication, a willingness to give up their own personal pleasure and convenience in order to make themselves available, so long as their elephants were on the picket line. When asked about the duration of this confinement, the elephant trainers admitted that they did get relief and relaxation when their elephants were confined to winter quarters.

One should be willing and capable of establishing ameable relationships not only with elephants, but with people who visit the zoos and circuses. Therefore, good public relations are essential.

Patience is a very important virtue. Practically every great elephant trainer interviewed by the author stated that patience was probably the most important human attribute for success in elephant training. Elephant training is a very slow process, and to be able to bear annoyance, provocations, misfortune, pain, lack of progress, and countless repetitions without complaint or loss of temper is very rewarding in the end. To be able to cope with such frustrations without unreasonable irritation, reflects insight and understanding of elephants which results from self discipline during years of experience.

Not everyone interested in being associated with elephants may possess the personality characteristics described here, but the motivation to aspire to achieve them will enhance one's enjoyment of their work, feel pride in accomplishment, and experience contentment with one's relationship with elephants.

Most of the great elephant trainers appeared to possess many of the characteristics described herein. It is hopeful that those persons who contemplate a career in elephant training give these matters serious consideration.

CHAPTER 9

THE ELEPHANTS

Among the vertebrates, elephants are scientifically differentiated in the Class Mammalia; Order Proboscidea; and Family Elephantidae. Paleantologists claim that 352 species of Proboscidea existed since their origin about 50 million years ago, but only two species survive today. The two living species are the African elephant, *Loxodonta africana* (Blumenbach, 1797,) and the Asian elephant, *Elephas maximus* (Linneaus,1758.) Among the african elephants two subspecies are recognized as *Loxodonta africana africana*, the bush or savannah elephant, and *Loxodonta africana cyclotis*, the forest or "pygmy" elephant.

Seven living subspecies of the Asian elephant have been described as:

Subspecies			Country of Origin
Elephas maximus maximus			Ceylon (Sri Lanka)
,,	,,	dakhumensis	Peninsular India
,,	,,	bengalensis	Northern India
,,	,,	birmanicus	Burma
,,	,,	hirsutus	Malaya
,,	,,	sumatranus	Sumatra
,,	,,	borneensis	Borneo

However, these subspecies are difficult to ascertain or distinguish in captivity. Owners of elephants in America do not generally know the subspecies of their animal, except to refer to them as Asian in distinguishing them from the African species.

DISTINGUISHING CHARACTERISTICS OF THE ASIAN AND AFRICAN ELEPHANTS

The African Elephant:

The most notable feature of the African elephant is the enormous size of the ears which often exceed the width of neck. The shape of the back is concave, or frequently referred to as sway or saddle-back. Both sexes possess tusks; males have larger, thicker tusks and females have more slender ones. The tip of the trunk has two "fingers." The less conspicuous features are: four toe nails on the forefeet and three on the hind feet. The skin is coarse and rough with tough bristly hairs. The trunk skin is ringed with deep fissures in the skin. The molar teeth are lonzenged shaped.

The Asian Elephant:

The major external characteristics of the Asian elephant include: relatively small ears; a convex or "hump" shape of the back; tusks more frequently found in males, but when present in females undeveloped in size; one "finger" on the tip of the trunk; five toe nails on the forefeet and four on the hindfeet; and size and shape of the head distinctly different from the African with anterior-posterior compression in the mid-line and conspicuous bulges on the dorsal aspect of the head. Less conspicuous features include: smooth skin with various spots and pinkish coloration; smooth trunk skin; and parallel and transverse dentine of the molor teeth.

In North America during 1978, the population of elephants in captivity consisted of approximately 215 animals: 86 of them were African and 119 were Asian, and they were located in 96 zoos. An additional 270 elephants were owned

Fig. 31 A male African elephant.

Fig. 32 A female Asian elephant.

by circuses and in private holdings. No data was available as to the subspecies or sexes in this census of elephants. Therefore, the total elephant population in captivity was 497 animals. Seventeen other countries held 66 elephants in 23 institutions. Thus, there is approximately a total of 724 known elephants in captivity throughout the world. This figure, however, is not entirely accurate as all the countries and institutions have not been accounted for, and there are undoubtedly many private elephant holdings that have not been reported. A recent survey in Africa estimated that the population of wild elephants was approximately 1,350,000. There are approximately 30,000 wild Asian elephants remaining in the world.

CHAPTER 10

THE BULL-HOOK

The enormous size and weight of elephants made it necessary for the early caretakers and trainers to devise some instrument that would aid in the control of these huge animals. At first, spears were devised and used. These consisted of long wooden shafts that could be easily handled and they had a sharp point on one end. In jabbing the tough, mud-encrusted skin, the pointed end of the wooden shaft frequently became dull and ineffective. Then a sharp metal point was attached to the end of the wooden shaft. However, the metal-pointed, long spears soon became unwiedly after the elephants were trained. The length of the shaft had to be shortened so that it was more manageable. Also, the pointed end of the shaft had to be modified so that the elephant skin could be hooked and pulled toward the trainer. Consequently, the modern bull-hook evolved and some are shown in the accompanying photograph.

The bull-hook is an indispensable instrument in the training and control of elephants. It is through the combination of spoken words and the effective use of the bull-hook that the trainer, handler or caretaker controls an elephant of any size. When not in use, the bull-hook should always be placed in the same conspicuous, convenient and accessible place where it can be readily obtained if necessary.

In using the bull-hook, the sharp points should not be deeply embedded into the elephant's skin, as it can readily

101

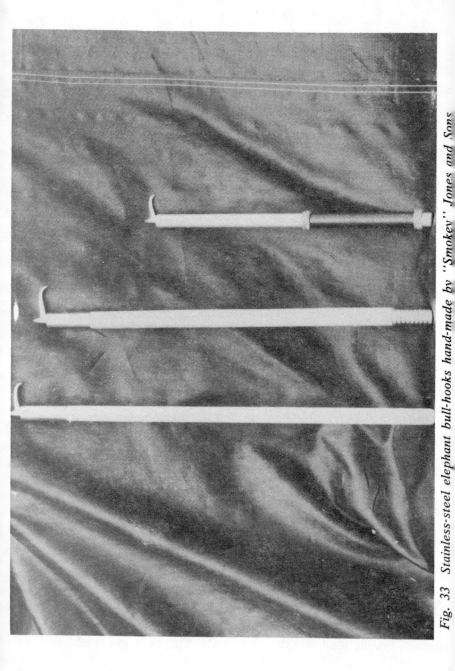

Fig. 33 Stainless-steel elephant bull-hooks hand-made by "Smokey" Jones and Sons

produce wounds that may become infected and difficult to heal. The sharp point of the bull-hook should be repeatedly jabbed into various places of the skin in a given area and not in the same place continually. The skin of the elephant is relatively sensitive, so it does not require deep penetration to obtain a response. After a period of effective training, simply placing the bull-hook on the skin will bring about the desired behavior of the elephant.

There are some places on the body of the elephant where the bull-hook should not be used. The sharp points of the bull-hook should never be jabbed into the top of the elephant's ear where it is attached to the head. Breaks in the skin at this point are difficult to heal because of the constant movement of the ears. The bull-hook should not penetrate the soft tissue around the elephant's eyes, mouth, and genitalia.

There is an old adage among great elephant trainers regarding the use of the bull-hook which states: "Not how much, but when." This implies that the bull-hook should be utilized as an aid to guiding and directing the behavior of the elephant. Only in certain rare instances should the use of the bull-hook be justified as an instrument to inflict pain or used as a weapon of attack upon an elephant. One of these instances might be when the life of a human being is at stake.

The metallic sharp points of the bull-hook should be made of stainless steel. This metal is resistant to rust, and it is easy to keep clean because of its smooth surface. Other metals are subject to corrosion and pitting in the metal where dirt and bacteria could accumulate and cause skin infections when the sharp points pierce the elephant's skin.

CHAPTER 11

COMMUNICATION

Elephants in their natural habitat are social animals, generally living in herds of various numbers of individuals of different ages and sexes. It must be inferred that there is some form of communication among the members. Elephants utilize several methods of communication including olfactory, auditory, visual and tactile. The trunk plays an important role in the execution of three of the four methods of communication between elephants. Elephants have a keen sense of smell and, frequently raise the trunk like a submarine periscope and sniff the air in search of olfactory information. The potential sources of olfactory information among elephants are the body odors, urine, feces, and the secretions from various bodily orifices such as from the temporal glands, penis, vagina and the anus. The most commonly occurring behavior among elephants is the manipulation of the trunk to the most likely sources of olfactory information. An olfactory sample of the odorous material is inhaled into the trunk to the most likely sources of olfactory receptors in the nostrils which pass on the information through the nervous system to the brain for final analysis. Both the African and Asian elephants also have two small openings in the roof of the mouth which are thought to be the Jacobsen's Organ. Reptiles obtain olfactory information from their environment by extruding the bifurcated tongue out of the mouth and passing it over their Jacobsen's Gland in a similar location in the mouth. It is deduced from the behavior of elephants that the Jacobsen's Gland might indeed be functional and play an important role in the analysis of certain olfactory information. Elephants were frequently observed placing their trunk near odoriferous parts of the body of another elephant, or on other smelly material, and then placing their trunk into their own mouth apparently utilizing their Jacobsen's Gland in analyzing the odor.

The trunk is also the primary organ in communication via the tactile sense. Actually, the sense of touch is clearly related with the sense of smell, as the trunk is the organ in common use. These two senses play a combined role in the feeding habit, since elephants obviously cannot see what they are about to eat and thus the trunk provides the avenue for tactile and olfactory information. Among the first signs that one elephant is aware of the presence of another is the extension of the trunk toward another elephant. Upon making contact, there is mutual exploration of one another with the placement of the trunk most frequently to such body parts as the mouth, ear, eyes, temporal glands, anus, tail and genitalia. The trunk is also used by mother elephants to caress, fondle and guide their young, and to discipline an unruly offspring. The trunks are intertwined during play-fighting among juvenile elephants and during more aggressive behaviors among male adult elephants. The trunk is also used as a weapon in striking at other animals or elephants in the vicinity, or even a caretaker or trainer. It is readily apparent that the trunk is a very useful and versatile organ for elephants, and care must be taken so that the trunk is not injured during training maneuvers.

Although there has been little or no experimental evidence to ascertain the visual acuity of elephants, it is generally believed that elephant vision is fairly good only at close ranges. Therefore, we may assume that visual signals are conveyed during interactions among elephants. The position of the head, the ears, and the trunk obviously give a certain amount of visual information to elephants in a group or between two elephants. The most conspicuous visual signal during mild excitement or more serious arousal is the extension of the ears at 90° angle from the axis of the body. This posture makes the elephant look larger than usual. In a serious elephant charge, the ears are extended laterally, the head held low, the tusks pointed at the adversary, and the trunk turned in ventrally under the head. An alert caretaker, handler or trainer will do well to remember this elephant posture.

Elephants are known to have a varied repertoire of vocalizations which consist of trumpets, growls, snorts, squeeks, rumbles, and roars. Each of these can be modified in a variety of ways. The sounds are emitted from both the trunk and the mouth. Just what each of the sounds mean has not been ascertained. Nevertheless, it is obvious that the vocalizations do convey information to other elephants although we have not as yet deciphered the code.

There have been some written accounts of "tummy rumblings" which have been allegedly heard eminating from wild elephants. More recent investigations of these alleged noises revealed them to be a form of purring sound, which apparently is not related to the digestive system. When wild elephants are out of sight of each other while browsing in the bush, they keep in communication by the purring sound. In case of approaching danger to any elephant in the herd, the purring stops and the sudden silence alerts the members of the herd. This purring sound has been reported among elephants in captivity.

Through the senses of smell, touch, vision and audition, elephants learn to convey and perceive certain signals and signs not only from each other but from their environment as well, that make herd life harmonious and make elephants aware of intruders. The young learn what to eat and how to behave by imitating their adults. Although the adult elephants are very tolerant of the mischievious antics of the very young and the disruptive activities of the juveniles, they do not hesitate to communicate their displeasure either by vocalizations or by a kick with the foot, a flick of the trunk, or a jab with the tusks.

Through a well established line of communication, a dominance hierarchy is established in an elephant herd. Each elephant soon learns its place and responds to the signs and signals of the leader of the herd, usually the biggest female. A correct response to the matriarch's signals has survival value in times of danger. Whether to signal the formation of a protective circle, to charge the adversary or intruder, or to leave the scene of danger depends upon the sagacity of the matriarch and her ability to communicate with other members of the herd. It is obvious that this system of communication has worked efficiently because elephants have adapted very well to their changing environment.

One of the most important characteristics in the training of elephants in captivity is the conveying of information between the trainer and the elephant. A line of communication must be established, utilizing the same senses of touch, smell, vision and audition, so that the elephant obtains some idea of what it is that the trainer wants done, and the trainer must have some feed-back from the behavior of the elephant as to whether or not the desired behavior can be executed. Although elephants are considered to be highly intelligent, there is no evidence that they understand the meaning of words. What these animals do learn is the sound of words that are associated with certain behaviors through the process of conditioning. The elephant learns to associate a certain command and its behavior because these have occurred contiguously in time. Therefore, in training elephants, single words or short phrases should be utilized instead of long sentences or conversations. Elephants can learn a large number of commands and it is seriously recommended that a uniform standard vocabulary be used by all elephant caretakers, handlers and trainers, at least for the basic commands. Adoption of a standard vocabulary of elephant commands will make the care, management and training of elephants more consistent, easier to learn by the animals as the elephant persons change from time to time. A standard vocabulary may also prove beneficial in times of emergency when elephants may have to be moved in a hurry.

The following words and their meanings are recommended as standard vocabulary in the care, management, and training of elephants in captivity:

Word or Phrase	Meaning
1. Alright	Resume previous status, e.g. stand up from laying down position, lower raised leg, etc.
2. Back-up	Move to the rear.
3. Bull	A male elephant.
4. Bull Hand	A person, usually in a circus, who is engaged in feeding, cleaning, moving or preparing elephants for shows.
5. Bull-hook	An instrument used to convey tactile information to an elephant.
6. Calf	A young elephant.
7. Caretaker	A person who feeds, waters, and cleans up around elephants.
8. Come here	Move to the left, or approach trainer when at a distance.
9. Come in line	Turn to the left and line up side by side.
10. Cow	Female elephant.
11. Easy	Move slowly, carefully, when passing through doorways, narrow places, or when stepping over objects.
12. Foot	Raise designated extremity.
13. Get over	Move to the right.
14. Go play	Move away from trainer in a free ranging area.
15. Handler	A person who can train or manipulate a "broken" elephant.
16. Lay down	Lay down on left side.
17. Lift	Raise designated foot higher.

18. Move up	Advance forward.
19. No	Negative command, unacceptable behavior.
20. Picket line	An extended chain to which elephants are secured by a forefoot and/or a forefoot and a hindfoot. Also, elephants chained up in a row.
21. Punk	A colloquial expression for a young elephant.
22. Stand	Assume standing posture on hind legs only.
23. Steady	Stop, remain in assumed position.
24. Trunk	Place trunk on forehead in S-Shape.
25. Trainer	A person who can take a wild or "green" elephant, teach it to respond to commands, put together an elephant act, or to control an elephant.
26. Tail up	Grasp the tail of a preceding elephant with the trunk.

Additional words can be added to these basic commands to suit the trainer in putting an act together, or in various other circumstances.

The caretaker, handler or trainer always "works" or commands the elephant from the left side of the animal. His position should be slightly ahead of the elephant's left leg.

CHAPTER 12

ANATOMY AND PHYSIOLOGY

The Skeletal System

The elephant's skeleton is comprised of a total of 210 major bones, which are distributed as follows:

No. of Bones	Structure
2	Head and mandible (lower jaw)
68	Spinal vertebrae
42	Ribs
1	Pelvis
2	Scapulas (shoulder blades)
44	Both forelegs (manus)
50	Both hindlegs (foot or pes)
0	Clavicle (collar bone)
210	TOTAL NUMBER OF BONES

These are the actual number of bones one would find in dissecting an adult elephant and this total does not include the fused bones of the skull and pelvis, nor the ossicles of the middle ear.

The elephant's skeleton is a remarkable feat of structural engineering. The bones of the anterior and posterior extremities have developed into sturdy, solid, upright supports for the enormous weight of the body. The vertical articulations of radius, ulna, and humerus of the forelegs as well as the tibia, fibula, and femur of the hindlegs make these extremities appear like formidable pillars. This skeletal arrangement makes it impossible for the elephant to jump or run like a horse or antelope. During the elephant's locomotion, the stilt-like extremities are prevented from being jarred from their sockets in the scapula and the pelvis by the absorption of the shock provided by the semi-digitigrade (in the forefeet,) and the semi-plantigrade (of the hindfeet) position of the bones of the feet which are cushioned by fibrous and fatty tisue in the soles. Elephants literally stand on their "toes" and "fingers." The soles of the forefeet are nearly circular, whereas those of the hindfeet are oval shaped. This unique structure does not impede the remarkable acrobatics accomplished by elephants as seen in circus acts.

There is a clear distinction between the skull of the male and female African elephants which can be noted even from a distance. In the first place, the skull is larger in the bull as compared to that of a cow of equal age. The most conspicuous difference between the sexes is that the top of the skull of the bull is rounded and it curves outwardly and then gently to the base of the trunk. In contrast, the top of the skull of the cow comes to a sharp peak and the forehead is more flat than rounded as it curves to the base of the trunk. These distinctions are more conspicuous when viewed from the side. Also, since the tusks are usually larger in bulls, the maxilla and pre-maxilla areas, which hold the tusks, are larger and broader than in the cow elephant.

The skull is almost indistinguishable between the sexes among the Asian elephants. However, the skulls are different from the African species by being more compressed longitudinally, rounded on top, and the forehead is more like that of the male African elephant. Seen from the back, the Asian elephant skull is broader than the African species.

An unusual feature of the skull of both the African and

Asian species of elephants is the extensive honeycomb-like spaces in the cranium. These air-filled pockets make it possible for the elephants to grow a large but comparatively light skull which is necessary for the attachment of the numerous muscles which are required to hold the head up, and to support the excessive size and weight of the tusks. Also, the pneumatized bones give the skull buoyancy when elephants are submerged in water.

The average weight of the skull in adult elephants is approximately 115 lbs. Due to the enormous weight of the head and tusks, the neck, which consists of seven vertebrae, is necessarily extremely short. This makes it impossible for an elephant to turn its head far enough laterally in order to see behind it, and it must turn the entire body in order to observe what is going on at its rear. This skeletal limitation makes the elephant very vulnerable to attack from the rear. It also becomes very agitated if it is unable to ascertain the nature of activity at its backside. This may explain why elephants become very nervous and dangerous in unfamiliar environments. Those persons associated with elephants may well remember not to approach or work around the rear of elephants without first making their presence known. In spite of their weight and size, elephants are capable of extremely fast movements and they may attack an intruder approaching from the rear as a purely defensive gesture.

It is generally believed that the elephant's skeleton, including the skull, continues to grow throughout the life of the animal.

Elephants in captivity are frequently afflicted with arthritic and rheumatoid disorders which affect the bones and joints of the extremities. These diseases are attributed to confinement in damp and cold concrete floors, poorly ventilated housing facilities, and insufficient opportunity to walk for extended distances. These diseases are rarely reported in wild elephants who generally walk a lot.

The elephant's skeleton is indeed remarkably appropriate, not only for the enormous size and weight of the body it must support, but also for the incredible agility it is capable of demonstrating as a result of its intricate masculature and nervous system.

The Nervous System and Sensory Organs

The nervous system consists of the brain and spinal cord which activates the muscles, glands and certain organs of the body, and receives a network of sensory information from specialized receptors in the eye, ear, nose, mouth and skin.

The brain is located in the extreme posterior portion of the skull. The average weight of the brain of an adult bull elephant is about 10 lbs., and that of a cow elephant about 8 lbs., with an average volume of approximately 6,000 cc. There are numerous convolutions in the cerebrum and the cerebellum. Microscopic examination of the brain tissue reveals highly complex interaction of neurons. This suggests that elephants have evolved neural structures and mechanisms which account for their extraordinary intelligence and diversified repertoire of behaviors.

The cerebellum, located in the back of the brain, and highly developed, regulates balance and coordination. It is no wonder that elephants are capable of performing head stands, foreleg stands, hindleg stands and one leg stands with relative ease.

The ability and range of function of an organ in the animal body is correlated with the arrangement and relative size of the nerves associated with them. Therefore, from an examination of the nervous system and sensory mechanisms, we can infer the relative capacity and range of behaviors of the animal even though we may never have actually observed the behavior of the animal. It is on this basis that many conclusions have been drawn regarding the capacity of the following sensory modalities:

Olfaction:
The trunk or proboscus is the major organ of olfaction or smell. It is the elongation of the upper lip, and it has

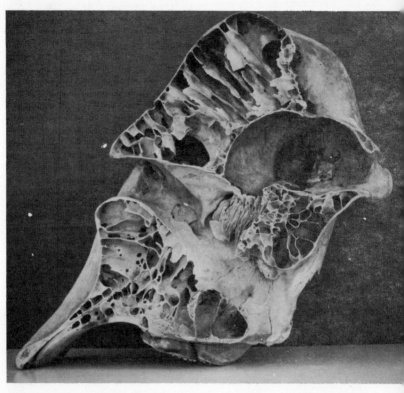

Fig. 34   Medial section of skull of female Asian elephant.

developed into a tube through which the animal breathes. The trunk is the most highly ennervated of all the sensory organs and, therefore, is capable of a variety of functions such as:

a. smell
b. grasping
c. sound producing
d. conveying food and water to the mouth
e. splashing the body with water, mud and sand
f. entertwining in play fighting
g. flexible
h. strength
i. caressing
j. highly tactile
k. effective weapon
l. manipulative and investigative

Vision:

Considering the large size of the animal, elephants have relatively small eyes. They are not greatly ennervated and thus vision is believed to be limited. Based on descriptions of elephant hunters, elephants are alleged to see better in dim light and are not responsive to color. This would imply that the retina of the eye would be dominated by rods instead of cones. If this could be supported by experimental evidence, then it would explain why elephants are nocturnal animals.

In addition to the upper and lower eyelids, the eyes are also protected by a laterally-moving, transparent, nictitating membrane. Although there are no tear glands, Harderian glands lubricate the eyes.

Gustatory:

The sense of taste is attributed to a liberal distribution of papillae on the tongue and the throat. The gustatory modality is highly sensitive, as any elephant trainer or caretaker has learned while trying to administer medication through the elephant's mouth.

The mouth is relatively small and the elephant takes exceptionally small morsels of food into it when feeding. Wild elephants average about 150 grams per mouthful of wet fodder. An adult female Asian elephant in captivity averages about 140 grams per mouthful of dry hay.

During an examination of the mouth, care must be taken to prevent the elephant from biting down on one's fingers. A ½" dia. x 6" in length, piece of dowling may be placed vertically in the open mouth to prevent it from closing. Also, a 1" x 6" board, about 12" long with a hole cut in the center large enough to pass the hand through may be placed horizontally on edge in the elephant's mouth to keep it open. These two methods simplify the examination of the mouth for abnormal dentition or for any other reason.

Audition:

The hearing mechanism is greatly ennervated and thus considered to be highly sensitive. Eight muscles control the movement of the ears. By placing the ears lateral to the body, sounds are directed toward the auditory canal and thus to improve hearing. This lateral position of the ears is also assumed during aggressive displays, making the elephant appear larger to an intruder.

Among wild elephants, with progressing age, the upper edge of the ears tends to fold over toward the body. Among elephants in captivity, the top of the ears tend to fold outwardly. In the latter case, this condition may be a significant symptom of debility, disease or malnutrition.

The pinna or ear flap contains an extensive network of blood vessels, and it is believed that movement of the ears cools the elephant's body by cooling the blood flowing through the ears.

The author has observed a male African elephant in captivity with an anteriorly prolapsed ear. Sylvia Sikes, a loxodontologist, attributed the condition to medial sclerosis of the arteries of the ear. However, in this case a spontaneous remission occurred after several months, so the condition may have been caused by injury or some other disorder.

Fig. 35 Male African elephant with "flop" ears.

117

The Circulatory System

The circulation of the blood through the body is achieved by means of the heart acting as a pump which forces the blood through arteries, capillaries and veins.

The elephant's heart is a four-chambered muscular organ which is located in the chest just posterior to the forelegs. The elephant's heart differs from that of other mammals in that it has two points at the apex instead of one. Another distinction is that there are two, instead of the usual one, (anterior vena cava) veins that return the blood to the right atrium of the heart. The average weight of the heart is approximately 24 lbs. It beats from 46-50 times per minute, and this can be felt at the base of the back of the ears. It has been noted that contrary to other animals, the heart beats faster when the elephant is recumbent than when it is standing. This may be attributed to the compression of other organs against the heart when the elephant is lying down.

The best place to obtain blood is from the back of the ear where the veins are very prominent. This also is the best site at which to administer intravenous medication.

The total amount of blood in the elephant's body has not been determined. However, the various components of the blood chemistry have been ascertained. There are about 3.5 million red blood cells per ml., and 10.5 thousand white blood cells pe ml. of blood. The blood has also been analyzed for various other chemical components. Research will have to be conducted to establish normal standards. This would be a great aid in time of sickness or disease among elephants.

The Digestive System

The Mouth:

The beginning of the digestive system is the mouth. The elephant's mouth is relatively small, and it is not capable of being opened very wide. The tongue is large and relatively mobile even though it is totally attached on the bottom side, a feature making it impossible for the elephant to protrude its tongue beyond the lower lip.

The upper or dorsal surface of the tongue is smooth to the touch, a quality attributable to densely packed projections called papillae. The tongue is a pinkish color with a variety of different types of papillae at different locations. Filiform papillae, which are the smallest in size, are located on the anterior or tip of the tongue. The fungiform papillae, which are medium sized, are located in the middle of the tongue. The foliate papillae, also medium sized, are located on the side of the tongue. The circumvallate papillae, which are largest in size, are located in the posterior or back of the tongue. According to sensory physiologists, mammalian taste qualities are related to various parts of the tongue: salt sensitivity is greatest on the top and side, sour also on the sides, sweet on the tip, and bitter on the back. It is presumed that these gustatory sensitivities are also characteristic in the elephants.

There is no uvula on the palate of the oral cavity.

There are the usual three pairs of salivary glands which are common to most ungulates, namely the parotids, sub-maxillary and the sub-linguals.

Dentition:

The teeth of elephants consist primarily of molars and incisors. The latter are frequently referred to as tusks. Elephants normally have six sets of molars in a lifetime. There is one molar tooth in each half of the maxilla and the mandible. A molar consists of a hard substance known as cement. On the occlusal surface of the molar are a number of elevated lamellae comprised of enamel which are surrounded by cement. The inside of the lamellae consists of dentine or ivory. The number and width of these lamellae represent the factors considered in estimating the age of the elephant. The lamellae are lozenged-shaped in the African elephant and parallel in the Asian elephant. These transverse ridges or lamellae constitute the grinding surface on which food is masticated. The development of Asian elephant molars suggests that the selection of herbiage as food is of a more delicate nature such as leaves and grasses, whereas the African elephant molars are capable of grinding more course materials such as bark, roots and branches.

Unlike other mammals, elephants have a unique origin, growth and replacement process of their molars. The molars originate in the back or posterior part of the upper and lower jaws, and they move forward to the front of the mouth and ultimately break off and fall out. During the molar replacement process, there are sometimes two molars in each quarter jaw. Due to various unknown causes this gradual replacement of molars may be interrupted. This interruption of molar progression may cause the elephant considerable pain. Abnormal aggressive behavior of the elephant may also be attributed to dental abnormalities. It is important to regularly examine the teeth of elephants in captivity. If normal progression of the molars is impaired, it may be necessary to physically remove the old molar so that the new one can develop normally. The sixth set of molars appear at about the age of 30 years and remain for the rest of the elephant's life.

When the elephant chews its food, the lower jaw moves in a forward and backward motion. This grinding movement ultimately wears out the lamellae and leaves the last set of molars perfectly smooth. This condition impairs the efficiency of masticating rough foods, forcing the elephant to seek soft and luscious vegetation usually found on the banks of rivers or lakes. This is where the old elephants with worn molars remain most of the time in order to survive. They eventually die there, and their bodies sink into the marshes and muddy banks. During draught years, the skeletons may be exposed and this adaptive behavior may have given rise to the myth of an "elephant grave yard." If such soft vegetation is not available, as in the time of drought, the elephants usually die of malnutrition because of the inability to masticate coarse and dry foodstuffs. In captivity, such a fate may not be experienced by the aging elephants because nutritious food which does not require grinding action in the

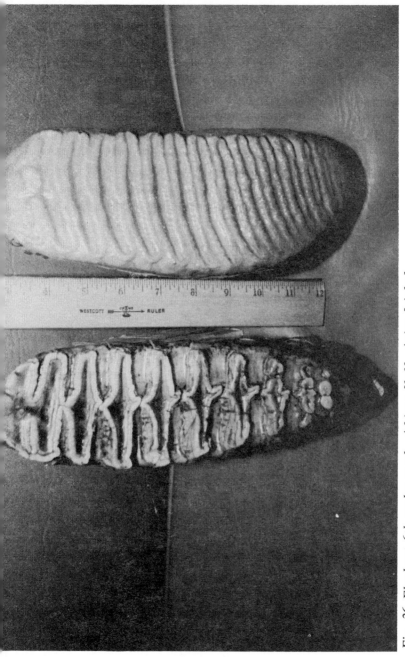

Fig. 36 Elephant 6th molar teeth, African [left], Asian [right.]

mouth may be supplemented in the diet, and thus prolong the life of the elephant.

Elephants in captivity occasionally develop cavities in their molars, and this condition may contribute to their mean dispositions.

The other component of the elephant dentition consists of the tusks which are overgrown incisor teeth which comprise the much sought-after ivory. There are usually two tusks, one in each part of the upper jaw or maxilla. Some specimens of elephant skulls in the museums of Europe and America consist of three and four tusks. Both the male and female African elephants develop fairly large tusks. In the Asian species of elephants, only the male elephants grow large tusks whereas the females develop only relatively small tusks referred to as tushes. Elephants of both species may develop to maturity without tusks. The heaviest tusks ever recorded weighed 235 pounds each. The longest tusks measured 11½ feet. Tusk size is related to age, genetic predisposition and available nutrition. Tusks of female African elephants grow long and slender, while those of males are thicker. There are very few wild elephants with very large tusks remaining today. Most of the big tuskers have been shot out for their ivory and presumably so have the genes for large tusks. In recent times, the most famous tusker was Ahmed who lived in the Marsabit National Park in Kenya. He died in 1974 at the age of 55. His tusks weighed only 148 pounds each, which were far from a record size. Tusks seen at ivory auctions today weight about 40-60 lbs. on the average.

The ivory tusks of African elephants are not as brittle as that of the Asian species and are, therefore, preferred for carving. Years ago, elephant ivory was used for billiard balls, piano keys, knife and pistol handles. This practice has been abandoned because of the scarcity of ivory and its high prices. However, ivory is still in great demand and thousands of elephants are killed illegally each year to supply the insatiable market for carved ivory jewelry, figures and ornaments. Because of its scarcity, ivory is becoming as valuable as gold, silver or gems.

Elephant tusks continue to grow throughout the life of the animal at the rate of about two inches per year. To mitigate the killing of the entire animal for its ivory, it is recommended that selected animals be anesthetized and their tusks harvested periodically like the wool of sheep. This practice would supply the demand for ivory and spare the animal's life.

The tusks are not used in the process of masticating food, however, they are used in digging up roots and tubers, and peeling bark off trees. Elephants show a preference for the use of the right or left tusk which becomes apparent by one being worn more than the other. The tusks are also used as weapons to impale an enemy. An elephant's tusk preference is important safety information when working with elephants.

Elephants in their natural habitat occasionally break off a portion of their tusks during fighting, digging, or debarking a tree. In captivity, tusks are usually sawed off because they can be formidable weapons when the elephant becomes aggressive. Elephants in zoos and circuses frequently break off large tusks by wedging them between the bars of their enclosures, or when they slip and fall on slippery pavements. Therefore, large tusked elephants are rarely seen in captivity.

The Stomach:

The elephant stomach is simple and it averages about 50-70 inches in length and approximately 20 inches in diameter in an adult. Its shape is similar to that of other mammalian herbivores. Based on the examination of the digestive organs in elephants killed in cropping operations in the National Parks of Africa, the stomach contents weighed on the average of 5-6% of the animal's live weight.

The Intestines:

The total length of the intestines is approximately 60 feet, of which the small intestine consists of about 46 feet and the large intestine of about 14 feet in length. The diameter of the small intestine is about 6-7 inches, the large intestine about 14 inches. Depending on the type of food eaten, it takes between 21 and 55 hours for food to pass through the digestive system of the elephant.

Other Digestive Organs:

There is a three-lobed liver which weighs about 90 pounds in an adult elephant. The pancreas is about 20 inches long and it weighs about four pounds. Elephants do not have a gall bladder.

The Excretory System

The kidneys are the major organs involved in the elimination of urine. One kidney is located on each side of the spine beneath the lumbar vertebrae. Their function is to filter out certain impurities from the blood that passes through them, and to eliminate them in the form of solutions which then flow through two ducts called ureters into a holding tank known as a bladder, to be excreted as urine through the urethra in a female and the penis in the male animal.

Depending upon the amount of water consumed and the temperature of the environment, an elephant usually voids urine approximately 12 times per a 24 hour period.

In normal health, the urine of elephants has a specific gravity of 1.003, its color is yellowish-amber, it is usually clear, it has a characteristic non-disagreeable odor, it is slightly acid, its flow is in a solid stream, and from 5 to 10 liters of urine are voided at a time. Some observers have noted that more urine is voided at night than during the daytime hours. However, if they are recumbent, elephants will stand up to urinate.

Disorder or disease of the urinary system may be suspected if one or more of the following conditions prevail:

Excessive dribbling of urine
Increased frequency
Decreased frequency or retention
Offensive odor
Any changes in the usual color

The urine is usually dark amber during a fever; reddish if mixed with blood; and greenish with a liver disorder.

Unusual behaviors during micturition, such as straining or groaning, frequent changes of posture such as lying down and getting up, crossing of the legs, and generally increased restlessness, may indicate a disorder of the urinary system.

The excretion of feces or solid waste from the body is described in the explanation of the digestive system.

SOME PHYSIOLOGICAL FACTS ABOUT ELEPHANTS

Age: The actual life span of elephants is not known. There is no accurate record of elephants in captivity living beyond the age of 60 years. The average circus elephant age is about 30 years.

Feces: From five to seven boluses are passed at each defecation, and there are approximately 15 defecations per day, with a total daily amount of about 250 pounds.

Food: An adult elephant may eat about 150 lbs. of hay per day. About 24 hours are required for the passage of the food through the alimentary tract. The digestive system is only about 40% efficient.

Gestation Period: The gestation period varies from 20 to 24 months. Baby elephants weigh approximately 200 lbs. at birth, and they are about three feet tall at the shoulder.

Height: The average height of adult elephants in captivity is about seven feet tall. Determining the height of elephants by twice the circumference of a forefoot is not a reliable measurement. There can be a deviation of from more than 12 inches to under eight inches from the actually measured vertical height at the shoulder.

Pulse: An adult standing elephant has a pulse rate of about 28 beats per minute, and the rate *increases* by about seven beats per minute when the elephant lies down. This is contrary to the condition in other mammals.

Respiration: The respiration rate of a standing awake adult elephant is normally about 10 times per minute. It is reduced to about half that rate when the elephant lies down.

Sleep: Elephants sleep soundly for about four hours, at about one hour intervals. They do take short naps while standing. They lie down to sleep between the hours of 1:00 and 4:00 a.m. if they are not disturbed.

Temperature: The normal elephant temperature ranges from about 94°F to 98°F or approximately 36.6°C. As a general rule the temperature is slightly higher in the evening and lower in the morning. One of the first symptoms of disease is a rise in temperature.

Urination: The average volume of urine in a single discharge by an adult elephant is about 1½ gallons, with a total daily volume of about 15 gallons.

Water: Elephants do not drink water through their trunk. They suck up about 1½ gallons of water into the trunk and let it pour out into the mouth as they raise the head and trunk. An adult elephant may drink up to 50 gallons of water per day.

Weight: The average adult circus elephant weighs about 6,000 lbs.

CHAPTER 13

REPRODUCTION

Elephant populations in their wild natural habitats are continually dwindling at an alarming rate. It is becoming increasingly apparent that if elephants are to exist at all, they will need to reproduce in captivity. However, since the passage of the Endangered Species Act in the United States in 1973, it is not permissable to import Asian elephants for commerical purposes, and African elephants have been placed on the Restricted List and their importation is regulated by a government agency. Therefore, the propagation of elephants in captivity will depend upon the successful reproduction among existing elephants in zoos, circuses and private ownerships. Unfortunately, elephants do not readily reproduce in captivity. In addition, there is an added problem in that there are only a very few known breeding male elephants in captivity, and the irony of it all is that at the present state of our knowledge only a male elephant can determine when a female elephant is in estrus. And the final tragic state of affairs is that the survival rate of elephants born in captivity is appallingly low. Therefore, the future abundance of elephants in captivity appears to be dismal unless something is done immediately. It is imperative that scientific studies be accelerated to ascertain the necessary and sufficient conditions for successful reproduction of elephants in captivity.

Very little is known about the mating behavior of elephants in their natural wild habitats. Ordinarily in the wild state, when a male elephant reaches puberty at about

10-12 years of age, he is expelled from the female dominated herd. He may pair up with another male or he may join a loose group of 2-10 bulls. The bull elephants may select to remain on the periphery of the female herd or they may exist in bachelor groups. Sometimes male elephants are seen in solitary existence.

When a bull elephant occasionally visits a female herd, he places his trunk in the vicinity of the female's genitalia and he sniffs for olfactory sign of estrus. If a cow elephant is found to be in a state of estrus, the bull elephant may respond in several ways. There may be some preliminary courtship behavior which may include mutual trunk entertwining. The male may place his trunk over the female's shoulder or on her back, attempts may be made to bite the neck of the female, or the male may lay his chin on the female's back, and finally there may be attempts to mount the female.

During copulation, the male mounts the female from the rear, similar to all other four-legged mammals, and with full penile erection he attempts intromission. There is usually a conspicuous S-shaped flexture of the penis when it is fully unsheathed. There are no pelvic movements by the bull, instead the penis is capable of considerable mobility and intromission is attempted by a series of vertical and lateral movements of the penis. When intromission is achieved, ejaculation occurs immediately. The duration of the mount is frequently less than 30 seconds and intromission less than 8 seconds. There are on the average about two intromissions per ejaculation.

Successful copulation depends upon the cooperation of the female elephant. She must stand still and support a considerable amount of the male's weight with her back. Copulation may take place several times over a period of days while the female is in estrus, and it may occur with several bulls.

Scientists have not yet been able to ascertain when a cow elephant is in estrus, or its duration. It is hypothesized that African cow elephants ovulate at the end of the estrus cycle which is thought to last between 24 and 48 hours. However, data based on deep vaginal smears from a captive African elephant in the London Zoo indicated that the length of the estrus cycle was approximately 16 days. Several owners and trainers have reported a periodic copious mucous vaginal discharge for several days from their Asian cow elephants. They speculated that this secretion is associated with the estrus cycle and ovulation. However, the cyclicity of the vaginal discharge has not been confirmed, nor has a scientific laboratory or chemical examination been made of the mucous discharge. So the significance of the vaginal mucous discharge and its relationship to reproductive physiology of the elephant has not yet been established.

Some recent reports claim that sexual maturity and conception can occur in female elephants as young as 6-7 years of age, and that bull elephants as young as 7 years are capable of impregnating an estrus female. This precocious sexual virility is attributed to proper nutrition and optimum density of elephants in a given area.

In general, the mating behavior is essentially the same in both the African and Asian species of elephants. Breeding may take place throughout the year.

Considerable success in breeding Asian elephants in captivity has been attained at the Washington Park Zoo in Portland, Oregon. It was at this zoo where the first baby male Asian elephant was born in the United States that survived infancy and lived on to sire a number of offspring. The veterinarian claimed that except for various supplementary vitamins, no special diet or hormones have been used to induce breeding or pregnancy. It might be pointed out, however, that there is no human dominance over the male elephant and therein might be the secret to the male elephant's sexual virility. The bull and cow elephants were regularly allowed to remain together in the pachyderm enclosure. Copulation has been observed to take place as often as twice a day for four days.

A rare success in breeding African elephants in captivity has been reported by the recent birth of a baby elephant at the Louisville, Kentucky, Zoo.

Fig. 37 "Motty," a baby elephant allegedly born from the cross-breeding of an A
female and an African male elephant at the Zoological Gardens in Che
England.

It has been generally assumed that African and Asian species of elephants were genetically incapable of interbreeding. However, at the Upton Zoo in Chester, England, a male elephant was born on July 11, 1978, of allegedly a 17 year old male African father named Jumbolena and an Asian mother named Sheiba.

The young offspring of mixed parents had characteristics of both elephant species. It had large ears, deeply fissured trunk with one finger; the front of the head was flat but there were two domes on the dorsal aspect; and it had five toenails on the forefeet and four on the hindfeet. Unfortunately, the baby elephant hybrid died of apparent intestinal disorder four weeks after birth.

The author was fortunate to be in England and to see the unusual baby elephant while it was alive.

If the alleged conception did indeed result from a male African and a female Asian elephant parents, then we will have to revise our thinking about interspecies reproduction of elephants. It may be possible to selectively breed the best characteristics of both species as is done in many domestic mammals such as dogs, cattle, etc.

Because of the many security problems inherent in keeping male African and Asian elephants in captivity, considerable interest is currently being shown in the possibility of artificial insemination of estrus female elephants. Researchers at the Wellcome Institute of Comparative Physiology, which is associated with the Zoological Society at Regent's Park, London, England, have explored the feasibility of artificial insemination of African elephants. Semen was collected from a live but sedated bull elephant by a technique of electro-ejaculation using a rectal probe and a square-wave electrical generator.

Additional attempts were made at collecting data on the physiology of ovulation in an African cow elephant by inserting a probe high up into the urogenital sinus by a technician from a crouched position beneath the animal's abdomen. Although this technique was successful for a time, attributed primarily to the exceptional rapport between the elephant and the keeper-technician, the researchers were doubtful if it could be applied to captive elephants in general. As a matter of fact, that research had to be temporarily postponed because the female African elephant suddenly refused to continue to cooperate. Thus our knowledge of elephant ovulation and the appropriate time for artificial insemination is still incomplete.

Semen is also being collected by scientists from male African elephants shortly after being killed during culling operations in many National Parks in Africa. The semen is frozen and kept in a sperm bank for future use.

It may be that natural conditions will have to be simulated in order to breed elephants successfully in captivity. The author strongly maintains that proper nutrition and adequate inter-social behavioral conditions will play important roles in successful propagation of elephants in captivity. Considerable research needs to be conducted on the behavior and physiology of reproduction of elephants before their propagation in any significant way may be achieved in captivity.

CHAPTER 14

ELEPHANT DISEASES AND ABNORMALITIES

Wild African and Asian elephants in their natural habitats are usually in fairly good health, although cases have been found with ecto- and endo-parasites and infected conditions such as boils and hardening of the arteries. Elephants in captivity are much more subject to diseases and disorders than are elephants in the wild.

It is imperative that anyone charged with the care of elephants in captivity should be a keen and intelligent observer. While standing, elephants appear to be in perpetual motion. Their trunk, ears and body seem to be constantly moving. And, even when they lie down, there are frequent movements. Elephants are also usually very inquisitive, and they frequently explore anything and everything within the reach of their trunk. The elephants' movements and inquisitiveness are normal and signs of a healthy elephant. It is when these two kinds of behaviors are reduced, or cease entirely, that one can suspect a possible illness or abnormality. A high fever is also a symptom of illness. A temperature above 100°F is considered feverish and an indication of infection or illness. If the elephant repeatedly emits any sounds, it may indicate that the elephant is in pain. It is obvious that if the elephant does not eat or drink, or has diarrhea or constipation, one can suspect something wrong.

Most of the pathological conditions of elephants in captivity are related to environmental factors such as inadequate care and nutrition. Most of the following named diseases and abnormalities could be avoided by preventive maintenance.

The Skin:

Wild elephants usually take good care of their skin. Under normal conditions they take frequent baths and wallow in mud and then rub their bodies against tree trunks, termite mounds or large rocks, because they can't roll over on the ground. This treatment tends to keep the skin moist, elastic, flexible and relatively free of ectoparasites. Elephants also protect their skin from sunburn by staying out of the hot sun during the day. The mud packs also protect the skin from sunburn. If mud is not available, elephants will dust the skin with sand or cover it with grass or other vegetation. Healthy elephant skin is tight and flexible, and the elephant can flick it like a horse in response to irritating pests.

Unfortunately, most elephants in captivity do not have an opportunity to take care of their skin. Elephants in zoos and circuses seldom have access to sufficient water in which to bathe, to coat the skin with mud and sand, or a chance to rub their skin especially in areas inaccessible to the trunk. Consequently, these elephants are subject to a variety of skin diseases and disorders.

Depending on the temperature and where the elephants are usually kept, they will tend to cover the skin with whatever is available. Since hay is frequently provided as food, this material is usually tossed onto the back and head. Under the best of conditions, hay is usually contaminated with fungi, bacteria and eggs and mature insect parasites. The skin is normally highly fissured and these contaminants tend to settle in the crevices of the skin and multiply.

Elephants normally eat and drink a lot and, therefore, they eliminate proportionately in the form of feces and urine. This waste material eventually contaminates the hay if it is not removed immediately. Most elephants in captivity do not enjoy ideal husbandry. The hay that was tosed onto the back eventually falls off and into accumulated feces and urine.

The elephants gather up the hay saturated in urine and mixed with their own excrement and toss that mixture on their back. It can be readily seen that this behavior covers the skin with potentially infectious material. Also, elephants chained in one place usually lie down in their own excrement and further contaminate their skin. The bristly hairs on the skin of the back keeps the contaminants from dropping off. Therefore, the heat of the elephant's body incubates the parasitic eggs and the larvae and mature parasites bore into the skin and feed on the body fluids. These openings in the skin become infected with bacteria and cause boils. Puncture wounds from excessive use of the bull-hook, or wounds incurred from loading and unloading elephants into vans or rail cars, or from other causes further predispose the skin to infection and cause abcesses and ulceration.

It, therefore, becomes obvious that elephants in captivity will require daily skin care including bathing or hosing the skin with water and vigorous scrubbing with a stiff brush in order to remove the accumulated contaminants and to prevent infections and other skin disorders. Lack of attention to daily skin care will result in the elephant's skin becoming dry and warty-looking. In addition, the skin will lose its elasticity and droop, giving a "baggy-pants" appearance. These latter conditions can also result from a lack of oil in the diet.

Elephants exposed to hot direct sunlight for extended periods of time can become sunburned. The symptoms of this condition are the usual redness and peeling of the skin. Also, if elephants are permitted to remain exposed to direct sunlight for long periods of time, or subjected to high temperatures, they may suffer sunstroke or heat stroke which may endanger the life of the elephant if it does not have access to water for bathing or drinking. The symptoms of sunstroke or heatstroke are lack of response to usual commands, lack of muscular coordination, rapid breathing and finally collapse.

Sunburn can be prevented by providing elephants shade or giving them access to mud, water or sand. Sunstroke and heat stroke can be prevented by supplying the elephant with a copious source of water. The elephants will spray the water over their body to cool it. If adequate sources of water are not available, elephants are capable of regurgitating water from their stomach, sucking it up into the trunk, and spraying it over the body. If sunstroke or heat stroke is suspected, a veterinarian should be called immediately. In the meantime, some sort of shade should be provided for the animal. If the elephant is down in a crouched positon, it should be rolled over on its side and doused with cold water. Cold water enemas are also helpful. After the veterinarian administers the appropriate treatment, the elephant should be made to get up on its feet and kept in the shade until recovered.

Elephants sometimes develop sudden multiple swellings on the skin. It is not known what actually causes this condition, but it may be attributed to an allergic response to some foods or a generally run-down state of the elephant. With improved conditions and a change in diet the small swellings are spontaneously reabsorbed. However, large accumulations of fluid under the skin may require drainage by use of a hypodermic needle and syringe, or a more radical treatment of cutting into the area to effect drainage of the fluid.

Sometimes in spite of preventive sanitary care, elephants may develop abscesses and ulcerations of the skin due to excessive penetration of the skin with a bull-hook. Abscessed areas of the skin can be identified as tender spots that may be swollen and hot to the touch of the hand. Drainage of the abscessed area should be instituted by the application of compresses soaked in warm, saturated solution of epsom salts. Ulcerations of the skin should be thoroughly cleaned with warm soapy or detergent water and flushed with a strong antiseptic. Abscesses and ulcers should also be treated with appropriate antibiotic dressings that can be obtained from a veterinarian, or injected intromuscularly by him.

Elephants in zoos and circuses are frequently made to get

down on their knees and elbows onto solid surfaces such as concrete and asphalt pavements. These surfaces are hard and abrasive and they cause severe bruising and cuts of the skin. Also during loading and unloading of circus elephants, or during the performance of circus acts, elephants frequently bump into sharp objects or steel cables and acquire skin wounds and abrasions. Prompt attention to these injuries by maintaining sanitary conditions and dressings with antiseptics will prevent infections and enhance healing.

When elephants are chained up for long periods of time in one place, they frequently develop disorders of the skin on the inside of the rear legs and feet. Urine and fecal boluses dropping to the concrete or other hard surface splash onto the rear legs, seep into the fissures of the skin and cause irritation and infection. A symptom of this pathology is the frequent crossing and rubbing of the rear legs together by the elephant. This leg skin abnormality can be avoided by daily washing of the skin on the inside surface of the rear legs or at least giving the skin a good hosing with water to dilute the accumulated debris.

Elephant skin is sparsely covered with bristly hair; however, most of it is worn off as elephants rub their body on any solid object or structure. The back of elephants does not get rubbed very often, so the hair grows to a length of 1-3 inches. Since elephants have the habit of tossing hay and other debris on their back, the hair tends to hold the material there. Prior to circus acts, elephants are usually swept off to make them appear clean.

One way to keep the debris from staying on the back is to remove the hair without hurting the elephant. There are a number of chemical depillatories on the market which can be applied to the skin in the form of creams and/or liquids. These chemicals dissolve the hair and should be thoroughly washed off and kept out of the eyes. An oldtime elephant trainer used to singe the hair off with a blow torch. This can cause severe burns to the skin if the flame is applied too closely.

Elephants in captivity are commonly infested with various forms of ectoparasites, including lice, ticks and the larvae of various flies. These skin parasites usually invade areas of the body inaccessible to the trunk such as behind the ears, around the anus and other body cavities and under the tail, where heat and moisture are present. The symptoms of this skin disorder include local itching, irritation, and inflammation. Another sign of this skin disorder is the tendency of infested elephants to rub the invaded part of the body against various structures if given an opportunity. Indeed, elephant enclosures should have objects such as a large rock, tree stumps, or logs on which elephants can rub the itchy parts of the body and thus dislodge insect parasites.

Skin parasite infestations can be avoided by frequently bathing the elephant and scrubbing the usually affected areas with a stiff bristled brush. A common treatment in the past included dousing the skin regularly with neat's-foot oil. Domestic sheep, cattle and horses are also infected with similar ectoparasites, and currectly there are various medications available in the form of dips and sprays, and these would be effective for use on elephants.

Superflous tissue growths or warts are occasionally seen on elephant skin. Warts of large size usually are injured and infected. These tissue growths should be surgically removed to avoid being irritated. An elephant trainer used to remove skin warts on elephants by the application of fingernail polish until they disappeared.

The Feet:

Wild elephants seldom have foot problems because they usually walk long distances, they are careful where they step, they use their feet to dig in the soil, and they bathe regularly. However, diseases and disorders of the feet are probably the most frequently occurring problems with elephants in captivity. The most common pathological conditions involving elephant feet include: fungus infections of the soles, overgrown nails, cracked nails, overgrown cuticles, and foreign bodies embedded in the sole.

Fungus infection of the soles usually occurs on the hind feet of elephants, but it can also affect the fore feet. This abnormal state seems to occur under conditions where elephants are chained in the same place for long periods of time and forced to stand in their own excrement, or on excessively wet floors. This condition is equivalent to athlete's foot in humans.

Fungus infection of the feet can be avoided by chaining an elephant in an area where urine and water will tend to flow away from the elephant; giving elephants all the water they want to drink but not leaving excess water around so that elephants can play in it and slop it onto the floor; and maintaining optimum sanitary conditions in the vicinity of the elephant by frequent removal of fecal material and wet hay.

The treatment of choice for fungus infections is to keep the feet dry by chaining the elephant in a dry place. The fungus infection will usually clear up spontaneously under such a regime. However, if the condition persists, walking the affected elephant over a sandy area may help to wear away the fungal infection. Failing this, treatment by a veterinarian may be necessary.

Split sole or heel and overworn sole are additional pathological conditions of the feet resulting when elephants remain standing in water or in their own excrement for long periods of time. One may suspect these abnormalities if the elephant resists the usual commands such as "move-up, or move over," is reluctant to have anyone palpitate the soles, and is obviously lame when walking. The constant moisture causes the sole to soften, and since the foot expands as the elephant places its weight on it, the usually tough sole splits and the break in the tissue becomes infected causing the symptoms described.

Split sole or heel is treated by first removing the elephant to a dry place. After all foreign matter has been removed from the crevices, flushed out with an effective antiseptic solution, and the wound trimmed of dead tissue, it should be dressed with a good topical antibiotic. If the elephant cannot be placed in a dry place, it may be necessary to fashion "boots" on the elephant's feet after they have been property treated.

As mentioned for split sole and heel, standing in water or in its own excrement for long periods of time tends to soften the soles of elephants' feet. If the elephants are then made to walk long distances over coarse surfaces, the soles tend to wear more than usual and become tender. The result is lameness.

The usual treatment is, of course, removing the afflicted elephant to a dry place, and giving it a rest period until the soles harden again.

Elephants that are not allowed to walk around to any great extent on abrasive surfaces such as asphalt or on open earth, tend to develop excessive tissue growths on the soles of their feet. This condition may be followed by uneven wear of the soles. Therefore, elephants should be walked daily. If this cannot be achieved, it may be necessary to use a draw-knife and to trim the soles.

Elephants' toenails also need attention. If unable to walk daily or to dig in the dirt, elephants develop overgrown toenails. The nails extend beyond the sole of the foot, resulting in unusual shape and sometimes cracking. A contributing factor to the cracking of nails is excessive moisture to the feet. The treatment for split or cracked nails is a regular pedicure, that is, cutting back the excessive nail and filing with a rasp to remove sharp edges.

A related abnormal condition of this part of an elephant's foot is excessive growth or cracking of the cuticle. This is part of the skin directly above the toenail. Elephants perspire in this area and the salty perspiration tends to dry this part of the skin, causing cracking, tenderness and pain. Daily washing and sanitary conditions will inhibit cuticle problems. The regular application of lanolin, vaseline or oil to the cuticle will also avert cuticle disorders.

A common foot problem of circus elephants is that foreign objects get embedded into the soles of the feet. The walking of elephants from railroad sidings to circus sites or from the "picket-line" to the arena where the acts are presented predispose the elephants to step on pebbles or stones, glass, wire, nails and other small debris. Once the embedded objects enter the fissured soles, they tend to be forced deeply into the tissue. The condition usually goes unnoticed until the foreign matter has penetrated into the soft tissue and causes inflammation and lameness. Therefore, elephants that walk in public places should have the soles of their feet examined daily and foreign bodies removed before they incapacitate the animal.

Elephants can develop skin and foot disorders if they are not chained properly. Severe abrasions, wounds and infections can result. Chaining alternate feet should be a routine procedure. This is especially important regarding the hind feet. Elephants usually strain on their hind foot chain by leaning forward more than they do on the fore foot chain, and thus can cause skin problems.

Degenerative Joint Disease:

A condition seldom seen in wild elephants is degenerative joint disease in the legs, but this disorder is frequently seen in captive elephants. The afflicted animal moves very slowly and appears to be in pain.

Improper nutrition may be an important predisposing factor. Some veterinarians attribute degenerative joint disease in elephants to inadequate housing facilities of captive elephants. They claim that elephants forced to stand on hard, moist and cold concrete floors without an opportunity to exercise on a dirt surface, or an inability to use an injured joint, tend to develop degenerative joint disease.

This disease will have to be diagnosed by an experienced veterinarian and treated symptomatically. This disease is not common among captive elephants living in wild animal parks where they have large areas in which they can walk on soil.

Most of the elephant skin and foot disorders that have been described here could be avoided or reduced by proper care and preventive maintenance. Prompt attention to minor bruises, careful use of the bull-hook, and maintenance of sanitary and dry conditions around elephants will help prevent skin and foot disorders.

Dental Problems:

As described in a previous chapter, elephant dentition is unlike that of any other mammal. The usual process of molar replacement predisposes the animal to various dental problems. I have found many developmental molar abnormalities in wild African elephants that have been shot during elephant culling programs. The abnormalities consist of impairment of molar replacement by injury, infection, or other causes. Dental cavities are rare.

Elephants in captivity are subject to dental cavities, improper occlusion of the grinding surfaces, and impairment of molar replacement. Such abnormal dentition contributes to inadequate mastication of the elephant's food with consequent decline in health. Elephant aggressiveness and misbehavior may be attributed to a toothache! One of the symptoms of dental problems is that the elephant refuses to eat. Periodic examination of the elephant's molars is important to detect any developing abnormalities. This may be difficult to accomplish because the elephant cannot open its mouth very wide. The suggestions for examination of the elephant's mouth that were made in a previous chapter will facilitate the examination of the molar teeth.

The other kinds of teeth in the elephant's head are the incisors which grow out to be the tusks. Abnormalities seen in wild elephants include: multiple tusks in a single socket; penetration by a bullet and later overgrown; erratic or excessive curvature; irregular or impaired development; and broken or split tusks.

About one-third of the total length of the tusk is in the maxillary area of the elephant's skull. This portion of the tusk is hollow and contains a highly vascular cone-shaped nerve pulp which extends down into the exposed portion of the tusk. The length of the nerve pulp in the tusk varies with

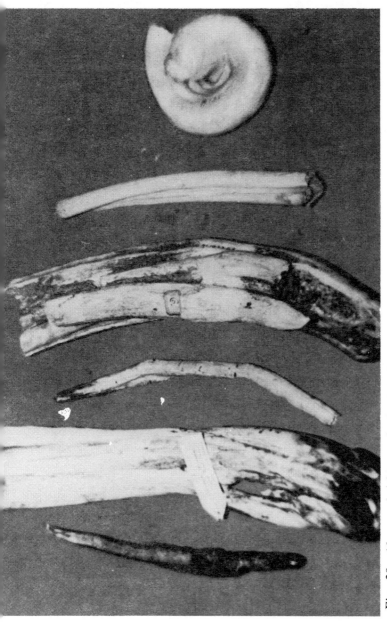

Fig. 38 Abnormal African elephant tusks.

143

the age, sex and species of the elephant. Immature elephants usually have longer nerve pulps in their tusks than do older mature elephants. The Asian species of elephants have relatively longer nerve pulps than the Africans, and females have longer pulps than males. Usually the anterior tip of the nerve pulp in the exposed tusk is about an inch or two longer than the distance from the base of the tusk to the bottom of the eye on the same side. Cutting the tusks off too close to the base can result in exposing the nerve pulp which may become infected and cause considerable pain. If this happens, the elephant will have to be anesthetized and root canal work performed by a dentist. The tusk nerve pulp may also become infected and inflamed if the tusk is broken off or split when the elephant falls on a hard floor, when fighting with another elephant, or by any other means. Jagged portions of broken tusks must be cut evenly and filed smooth to prevent further spliting and injury to the nerve or injury to another elephant by rubbing the sharp, jagged edges on the body of another elephant, or further damage to the pulp by catching the jagged, broken tusk on objects in the environment of the elephant.

The appearance of a black discoloration at the end of a cut or broken tusk may indicate a probable infection or hemmorrhage of the nerve pulp. This condition will have to be treated with antibiotics, and the tip of the tusks must be covered with epoxy cement or similar material, after prior sterilization of the area, until growth of new ivory occurs.

Diseases and Disorders of the Digestive System:

The incidence of diseases and disorders of the digestive system of elephants in the wild state has not been ascertained. Examination of some wild African elephants revealed varying amounts of pebbles and parasitic worms in the stomach. Bile stones have also been found in the liver duct.

The most common disorder of the stomach and intestines of elephants in captivity is parasitic worm infestations of these organs. Usually two kinds of Ascaris worms are involved. They are threadlike, white, and range from 0.5 to 2.5 inches in length. Most elephants harbor these parasites and their presence apparently causes no harm except when they multiply into large numbers.

The usual symptoms include debility, malaise, lack of appetite, and ill-health. It is believed by some experts that the eating of earth by elephants is an indication of worm infestation. The finding of large numbers of worms in elephant dung confirms the diagnosis.

The recommended treatment of gastrointestinal parasitism has been a daily ration of salt and internal medication. A very effective vermifuge for round worms in elephants, which has been used for years, is phenothiazine. A veterinarian can prescribe other effective remedies.

Another frequent gastrointestinal disorder is colic. The symptoms of this disorder include abdominal distention, restlessness, pawing of the ground with the forefeet, crossing of the hind legs, and occasionally biting of the trunk. The elephant may also frequently lie down and get up. This behavior suggests intermittant pain.

Colic is usually caused by: engaging the elephant in unusual bodily positions, drinking cold water, changing the diet radically, and/or ingesting certain rich foods such as watermelon rinds, green corn stalks, and clover hay, and infestation with large amounts of intestinal worms. The conditions may also be brought on by the consumption of large amounts of earth or sand which become impacted in the intestines.

A veterinarian should be called for the treatment of colic because it may be necessary to infuse large quantities of fluids introvenously, and analgesics may have to be administered to allay the pain. In the meantime, some relief may be obtained by instilling large amounts of warm soapy water enemas.

"Broken-heart," "Sudden and Mysterious-Death Syndromes:"

African and Asian elephants in their natural habitats are highly gregarious animals. Individuals in family or social groups form strong bonds between one another. They engage in considerable body contact and mutual fondling by means of the trunk. Solitary elephants are rarely seen. Elephants comfort and allay each other's anxiety under stressful and traumatic conditions by various sounds and by placing their trunk into each other's mouth.

Elephants in captivity have been reported to have died suddenly under mysterious circumstances without any apparent contributing pathology. This phenomena has been referred to as "Sudden-death" or "Broken-heart syndrome." This condition occurs more frequently among young elephants, but it has also been reported in mature adults.

Elephants are susceptible to gripping fear when they are separated from their customary family or social group, when placed in strange environments or enclosures without a companion, when there is a sudden change in caretaking personnel, when placed in solitary confinement, and when undergoing training.

Just why these conditions should precipitate sudden death is not clearly understood. One theoretical explanation is that an unexpected extraordinary stimulus or shock to the sympathetic nervous system may cause an excessive and unmitigated reaction of the sympathetic nervous mechanisms which prepare the bodily processes for flight or fight. Such a prolonged state of physiological events may trigger cardiac fibrillation, impeding the flow of blood to vital organs and causing death.

Whether or not this is the correct explanation for the sudden death syndrome remains to be confirmed. However, all elephant persons should be alerted that such a tragedy can occur and steps should be taken to prevent it. Elephants in captivity should be kept at least in pairs under conditions where they may touch bodies and trunks. If this is not possible, elephants should be regularly stabled with other animals with which they are familiar, or within the sight and sound of the caretakers. Caretakers should work as partners or teams so that in case of necessary change one or more persons will always be familiar to the elephant. Elephants should not be approached unexpectedly and silently from the rear. The approach should be made by previous sight or sound. Training periods at the outset should be of brief duration so that the elephant will have an opportunity to recover from the shock and trauma of training procedures.

The diseases and disorders of elephants that have been discussed up to this point, were pathological states which could have been avoided or significantly reduced by maintaining sanitary conditions around elephant quarters, providing proper and adequate nutrition, and giving immediate attention to injuries, cuts, and bruises. The recommended treatments are in the realm of common-sense and are suggested procedures that the elephant person could perform immediately to allay pain and discomfort, and to enhance the healing process in elephants suffering from certain diseases and disorders.

There are a number of other diseases and disorders such as those involving the circulatory system, the respiratory organs, the urogenital system, and the nervous system. The symptoms of pathology in these complex organs are often unknown or may require extensive examination by trained professional technicians or experienced veterinarians who may be required to administer special treatments involving drugs and sophisticated equipment. Therefore, a wise elephant person will constantly be on the alert and observant of sometimes very subtle changes in the behavior or health of the elephants entrusted to his/her care and management. The important thing to remember is to recognize the limitations of one's own capability and to seek professional help before an elephant disease or disorder progresses to an advanced state that may seriously incapacitate or endanger the life of the elephant.

Elephants in captivity have been known to die from the following causes: acute intestinal infections, complications resulting from surgery, cardiac arrest, brain tumors, injury from accidents, enteritis, pheumonia, calf white-muscle disease, sudden death syndrome, rheumatoid arthritis, septicemia resulting from any infection, especially poor foot care, acute explosive diarrhea, and euthanasia by lethal dose of drugs, gunshot wounds to the brain, heart or lungs, and by hanging.

CHAPTER 15

THE CARE OF ELEPHANTS

The care of elephants implies dedication, attention, towards and fondness of elephants. Any person who can measure up to this description may be designated as an elephant caretaker. Such a designation may include elephant owners, handlers, trainers and others with interest in elephants.

An informed elephant caretaker will be an efficient and happy one. One way to become informed is to read thoroughly not only the content of this book, but also many if not all of the literature cited in the bibliography at the end of this book, and to seek out other printed information on elephants. A second way to become informed is to ask questions of experienced elephant persons. A third way to become informed is through experience with elephants and to be keenly aware of what is going on.

An important aspect of the caretaking of elephants is to be a good observer, and to keep complete written records on the elephants one is in charge of.

If one has an understanding of the habits and lifestyles of elephants in their natural habitats, one can attempt to simulate as closely as possible those conditions in captivity, for the benefit of the elephants and the caretaker. Of course, the conditions of the elephant in the wild state cannot always be simulated in captivity, nor would it be advisable or desirable at times, but by studying the elephant in its natural habitat one can gain insight into the repertoire of behavior of elephants and thus understand them better in captivity.

An important point to remember when working around elephants is that they are not domesticated animals with hundreds of years of special breeding such as the genetically determined traits of horses for speed, cattle for milk or beef, and all the various traits of different breeds of dogs. Elephants are wild animals! Not only are elephants wild animals, but they are also the largest and strongest land animal in existence, and they have the always present potential for killing or injuring their caretakers and for demolishing most physical structures.

Even though elephants in captivity may appear to be trained and conditioned to respond appropriately upon command, they may revert at any time to instinctual behaviors which may be entirely unrelated to the behaviors learned in captivity. The instinctual behaviors are attributed to the specific defense reactions that have survival value for the animal in a natural environment. Elephants have not been studied in the laboratory as the white rat, so all the stimuli that are most likely to produce certain responses have not been ascertained for the elephant. Therefore, elephants are unpredictable in their behaviors, and they require constant alertness on the part of those to whom elephants are entrusted.

Newspapers have reported a rash of cases in zoos and circuses where elephants that have been apparently docile for many years and unpredicably turned on their caretakers, handlers or trainers and seriously injured or killed them. These actual cases should warn any elephant caretakers to be constantly alert, to avoid carelessness, and to constantly think ahead as to the likely probability of unexpected elephant behavior under various circumstances whether in a zoo, circus, or private ownership. Every wise and intelligent elephant caretaker should have a contingency plan, with all the necessary material and personnel readily available just in case an elephant should get out of control. It might be a good idea to hold emergency drills from time to time so that people around elephants become aware that the unexpected will be expected.

Asian elephants have been associated with human beings for a long time and numerous generations of elephants have been born in captivity. Therefore, Asian elephants are more docile and amenable to learning to respond to commands in various situations such as working in lumber camps in Burma and Thailand, and in circuses and zoos around the world. Asian elephants have thus readily adapted to the captive environments.

African elephants have not adapted to captivity as readily as the Asian species. Experiments in Zaire, Africa (formerly the Belgian Congo) involved attempts to train African elephants to do work in forests and agriculture. Some success was achieved in the early days of the project but today African elephants are rarely used in doing work in captivity in their native countries as is still done in Burma, Thailand and Sri Lanka with Asian elephants. Because of their relatively recent association with man in captivity, African elephants are more difficult to train. However, trainers who have successfully trained African elephants claim that they are more dependable and efficient in their performance than are Asian elephants. However, the behavior of male African elephants is very difficult to predict, and they frequently become unmanageable and, therefore, circuses have shied away from keeping male African elephants in their show acts, and those circuses that have owned male African elephants eventually donated or sold them to zoos.

Elephants in their wild natural habitat have been seen at the cold snow levels of mountains, but most of the existing elephants in the wild state live in areas located near the equator where the temperature is the warmest. Nevertheless, elephants are rarely seen out in the open sunshine at the highest temperature of the day. They usually take cover in forests or other shady areas during the day. Most of their movement takes place after sunset when the temperature is more moderate. At this time, they visit the waterholes to drink, mud and bathe.

What these observations of wild elephants tell us is that

elephants in their natural habitats avoid the extreme heat of the day. This gives us some idea as to the kinds of shelter to provide for elephants in captivity.

Although elephants are frequently named pachyderms, meaning thick skinned, their skins are relatively sensitive to sunburn and insect infestation. The application of mud to the body, and the tossing of sand onto the back, may be behaviors aimed at protecting the skin from the insect pests and from the heat of the sun. Therefore, elephants in captivity should not be kept in the open sun if they do not have an opportunity to apply mud or sand to their bodies.

Elephants cool their bodies by reducing the temperature of the circulating blood by flapping their ears. The temperature of the blood is 10-15°F cooler when it leaves the ears than it was when it entered the ears.

Another way elephants reduce the temperature of the body is by regurgitating water from their stomach, aspirating it with the trunk, and spraying the water over the body. Air passing over the moist body tends to reduce the body temperature.

Although Hannibal drove 37 elephants over the Swiss Alps to attack Rome in 218 B.C., only 12 elephants survived the ordeal. The elephant skin is quite thick over some parts of the body, and it is sparsely covered with hair. This lack of hair makes it difficult for the elephant to conserve body heat. Furry or heavily haired skins trap air and provide such animals with efficient insulation to protect them from frigid temperatures. Elephants do not have the benefit of hair or fur to protect them from adversely cold temperatures. They do not tolerate cold weather very well, especially when they are chained and cannot walk to generate heat. Elephants tend to weave or rock back and forth more often when they are cold.

Therefore, elephant shelters in captivity should maintain regular moderate temperatures of 65-70°F, if the animals are kept indoors. There should be adequate ventilation in the elephant enclosure. The optimum space for one adult elephant when immobilized is approximately 14' x 10' area.

The floor in the elephant enclosure should be constructed of concrete. There should be a sloping of the floor from the front to the rear of the elephant so that urine, water, and other liquids will flow away from the elephants. Adequate drainage should keep the floor relatively dry. This is to prevent foot infections and disorders. The shelter should contain a source of drinking water and a trough from which the elephant can drink the water. However, water should not be left in the troughs after the elephants have had their fill, because they play in the water and tend to keep the area unnecessarily wet. The water source should also contain an attachment for a hose of 30-40 feet in length with which to wash down the elephant if necessary, and to hose the waste into the drains.

Heating elements should be installed into the concrete floors. This will not only help to keep the floors dry, but it will provide heat to the body when the elephants lie down during cold evenings or during the winter in northern geographical area.

Steel rings should be welded onto sections of steel I-beams and then embedded into the concrete when the floor is poured. The top of the beam should be level with the floor. If steel rings are embedded directly into the concrete, a depression is worn around the ring, and these areas tend to collect debris, water and waste. The rings in the concrete floor should be 14'3'' apart in the longitudinal plane; that is, from the anterior to the posterior of an adult elephant which is to be chained in a given area. The size of the chain should be 3/8'' - 1½'' links. The length of the chain should be approximately 6'' overlapping the ends when the anterior and posterior chain is stretched out toward each other. The ends of the chain should contain clasps that cannot be unfastened by manipulation by the elephants.

The elephants should be chained first by a hind leg just below the knee, then commanded to move forward and chained by an opposite foreleg just above the wrist. The legs to which chains are attached should be alternated to prevent injury to the skin from repeated chaining on the same leg.

The storage of hay, grain and other foodstuffs should be nearby but out of the reach of the elephants. Adequate working space for preparing food should be allocated. Metal bins for grains, and other foods of that nature, refrigeration for perishable foodstuffs will minimize spoilage, odor and rodent and insect infestation.

Every elephant shelter should have an escape route for the caretaker in event the elephants become unmanageable.

Elephants kept outdoors should have some sort of canopy over them to protect them from direct sunlight and evening moisture.

Electric fences are of limited value in containing unchained elephants in a selected area. Elephants have been known to devise devious means of breaking out of electric-fenced areas.

Concrete moats around an outdoor elephant enclosure will contain the animals. However, although elephants usually will not step down below an area where their trunk will not reach, they have been known to slide down inclines on their buttocks or belly, and to dig away at the soil on the sides of ditches to such an extent until they could walk up the land barrier.

Chain link fences are easily destroyed by elephants. The only known fencing to contain elephants is that constructed of steel railroad rails and 1½'' steel cable which was installed at the Addo Elephant Reserve in South Africa.

Chaining elephants temporarily outdoors can be achieved by driving 4 foot long steel auto axel rods into the ground at 10 foot intervals in two rows. Chains are then stretched out in two rows, and the elephants chained to their front and rear legs between the parallel rows of chains. This method of securing elephants is known as the "Picket line" and is frequently used by circuses.

The Elephant Diet

Before the establishment of the national Parks in Eastern African countries, elephants used to congregate in the moist valleys during the dry season to feed on the succulent grass and variety of green brush, grasses, fruits and roots, and there was sufficient residual water in the streams and pans. About March of each year the vegetation began to dry out and the water disappeared. The elephant family groups broke up and dispersed and many elephants migrated to distant areas where heavy rainfall stimulated the growth of new grasses and plants. When the herds returned to the original valleys from their annual migrations about November, they found the local vegetation lush and luxuriant again and it adequately supported their numbers for the next several months. Thus, elephants utilized their habitat in a cyclic fashion and they instinctively selected the necessary vegetation to maintain their health under normal conditions.

With the creation of the National Parks in the 1940-1950's, the long migrations of elephants no longer take place. Elephants are confined within the boundaries of the Parks for the entire year. Their numbers have multiplied to the point where the vegetation in the areas the elephants inhabit can no longer support them. Consequently, hunger, thirst, and death result especially if prolonged drought is experienced in areas of heavy concentration of elephants. In Tsavo National Park, Kenya, during 1970-71, 5,900 elephants died of thirst and starvation.

Because of large populations in some areas and diminished quantity of natural herbiage, elephants have resorted to uprooting trees by knocking them over and feeding on the leaves and roots. The hungry elephants would also ignore Park boundaries and raid neighboring farmlands where they would destroy crops and terrorize the villagers. These raiding elephants were frequently killed by gunfire. The destruction of the trees has a marked effect upon the ecology of the Parks. If such trends were to continue, the elephants would probably destroy the source of their sustenance and eventually themselves. Consequently, many thousands of elephants are being killed each year in various National Parks of Africa in order to control the populations of elephants and to preserve the ecology of the Parks. With the increasing human populations in modern Africa, there is greater and greater demand for land in the name of human

Fig. 39 Native African workers skinning a portion of hundreds of elephants that were shot dead in a government elephant culling program.

industrial, agricultural and housing expansion. This trend, which is euphemistically termed progress, is responsible for creating further problems for elephants by forcing them to abandon their normal life-styles and habitats. The elephants are thus destroying the very sanctuaries that were intended to provide them protective security. In many National Parks in Africa, hundreds of elephants are being killed so that some may survive under the prevailing conditions.

Ironically, the United States Government has restricted the importation of African elephants because they are an endangered species; since thousands of elephants are being killed because there are too many elephants in some National Parks of Africa, the logic is beyond comprehension.

Fortunately, during the elephant cropping operations some important scientific information relative to the nutrition of African elephants has been obtained.

From stomach-fill data obtained from elephants cropped in the Murchison Falls area of Uganda, researchers estimated that the average daily consumption of vegetation in the wet season was 4.8% of body weight for males and 5.6% for females. Analysis of the stomach samples revealed that on the average there was 8.4 g. protein; 1.5 g. of fat; 43.5 g. of carbohydrate; 35.7 g. of fiber; and 11.0 g. of minerals in 100 g. of dry matter. Elephants eat 12 to 14 hours per day in order to obtain the necessary nutrients.

A 10-year old male elephant of approximately 4,000 pounds was observed for its feeding habit in the Tsavo National Park, Kenya. The elephant selected its diet from 28 botanical Families, and he browsed 64 species of vegetation. A study conducted in the Kruger National Park, South Africa, revealed that 101 plants were eaten by elephants.

The feeding habits of Asian elephants are remarkably similar to those described for the African elephant, both in the manner of feeding and in the amounts and types of vegetation ingested. The Asian elephant's teeth indicate that they consume vegetation which is not as coarse as that eaten by African elephants.

The Diet of Elephants in Captivity

Obviously, elephants in captivity cannot be permitted to forage for their food as they do in the wild state, except under special circumstances where large space and security make it possible to do so.

Unfortunately, animal nutritionists have not determined the precise dietary requirements for elephants. Therefore, our knowledge of the diet of elephants is extrapolated from the nutritional requirements that have been determined for domestic animals. The dietary requirements of elephants could be assumed to be similar to that of horses except for the extraordinary large size of elephants. Because of the huge size and weight of elephants, more food is required than for horses, not only for the basic homeostatic processes but for the physical activity such as walking, working or performing in circus acts. In other words, elephants have higher energy needs than horses. An analogy would be the gasoline consumption of a Cadillac motor vehicle compared to a Toyota. Because digestion in elephants in only 35-40% efficient, elephants do not obtain as much nutrition from their food as do other animals. Also, elephants do not possess the proper enzymes to break down cellulose, which is the major ingredient in elephant fodder. These factors must be kept in mind when feeding elephants.

The analysis of the stomach contents of elephants cropped in their natural habitats, suggests that the optimal daily food requirements are approximately 6% of live weight on a wet food basis and approximately 1.5% on a dry weight basis. Assuming that an average elephant weighs 3,400 pounds, then the average daily food requirement would be about 204 pounds of wet vegetation or 51 pounds of dry food. A larger or smaller elephant would, of course, require more or less food, respectively. Also, food requirements will vary with conditions such as maintenance growth, reproduction and lactation, and the activity of the elephant.

Of the 51 pounds of dry food required by an average elephant weighing 3,400 pounds, 4 pounds should be in proteins; 1 pound of fat; 22 pounds of carbohydrates; 18 pounds of fiber; and 6 pounds of minerals.

The source of these nutrients is usually the commercial preparations available in the form of hays, grains, and combinations of ingredients as dietary supplements. Alfalfa is a very important legume which is grown as hay. This hay contains a relatively high content (as high as 12%) of digestible protein. Other types of hay and their relative values of digestible crude protein are: barley, 5.2%; ryegrass, 4.8%; wheat, 4.4%; oats, 4.1%; and timothy, 3.6%. The percentage composition of protein in cereal grains is about 12%. Young leafy pasture grass has about 3.2% of protein. Groundnuts (peanuts) are a high source of protein, containing about 27% protein.

The percentage of fat is highest in tuberous root and groundnuts such as peanuts which contain about 45% fat.

The highest source of carbohydrates is found in cereal grains where their composition is about 71%.

Most of the foods provided in the form of fodder for elephants contain mostly fiber, so this constituent of the diet is most easily provided from the regular fodder.

Mineral elements required by elephants for normal health and growth are said to be in very small amounts. Research workers in the field of animal nutrition claim that more than 47 mineral elements may have important metabolic roles in mammalian tissues. Among the essential minerals are calcium, phosphorous, potassium, sodium, chlorine, sulphur, magnesium, iron, iodine, manganese, zinc, cobalt, molybdenum, selenium and chromium.

Deficiency in calcium produces a condition known as rickets, the symptoms of which include misshapen bones, enlargement of the joints, lameness and stiffness. Another condition found in adult animals and attributed to calcium deficiency is osteomalacia in which the calcium in the bone is withdrawn and not replaced. Consequently, the bones become weak and are easily broken. Green, leafy crops, especially legumes are good sources of calcium, whereas cereal grains and roots are poor sources of calcium.

Phosphorous is a mineral closely associated with calcium in animal bodies. Phophorous plays an important role in carbohydrate metabolism in the forms of various intermediate chemical reactions. A deficiency of phosphorous can cause rickets and osteomalacia. In cattle, a deficiency of phosphorous creates an abnormal alteration in the animal's appetite causing the affected animal to chew on wood, bones, rags and other foreign materials. Low dietary intake of phosphorous may also be associated with poor reproductive records of elephants in captivity. Cereal grains are good sources of phosphorous, but the phosphorous content in hays and straws is usually very low.

Potassium plays an important role in nerve and muscle excitability, and in the metabolism of carbohydrates. Deficiency in potassium caused paralysis in laboratory animals. The potasium content of most plants is generally quite high, so that it is normally ingested in larger amounts than any other mineral, and thus very unlikely that a deficiency might occur, except in extreme conditions.

Sodium is associated with potassium in the regulation of the acid-base balance and the osmotic conditions of the body fluids. Sodium is found mostly in the soft tissues and body fluids of the animal. Retardation in growth and the reduction in the proper utilization of the digestive proteins is attributed to a deficiency of sodium in the diet. Most foods normally ingested by elephants are comparatively low in sodium, so this mineral must be given in supplementary form such as common salt or salt licks.

Sulfur in the animal body occurs in proteins containing amino acids and vitamins. A deficiency in sulfur would also indicate a deficiency in protein.

Magnesium is the major enzyme activator in bodily metabolism. It is closely associated with calcium and phosphorous. This mineral has gained considerable attention in recent years among cattle ranchers because a deficiency in magnesium is reported to cause tetany and death in livestock. A condition known as hypomagnesemia affects ruminat cattle and the symptoms of the disease are often precipitated by conditions which cause the animal undue stress such as cold, wet and windy weather. This also applies to elephants. Apparently adult animals have a relatively small readily available reserve of magnesium in the body and consequently they may suffer a sudden depletion-causing symptoms. Therefore, magnesium must be obtained through dietary supplements.

The following named minerals are referred to as trace elements because they apparently are required in relatively small amounts for proper metabolic processes. Iron is a mineral that is combined with proteins, and it is also a vital component of many enzymes in the body. A dietary deficiency in iron affects the formation of hemoglobin in red blood cells and causes anemia. Excellent sources of iron are leafy green leguminous plants and seed coats. Cereal grains are a poor source of iron. Excess iron in the diet may cause digestive disorders and it interferes with the utilization of phosphorous.

Copper is a dietary essential mineral for the production of red blood cells and for augmenting their activity in the circulatory system. It plays a vital role in many enzyme systems, and it is necessary for normal pigmentation of the hair. The symptoms of copper deficiency include anemia, poor growth, skeletal disorders, diarrhea, gastrointestinal disorders, and lesions in the brain stem and spinal cord. Copper is usually widely distributed in various foods under normal conditions. Because excess copper in the animal's body is toxic, considerable care is required in supplementing the elephant's diet with copper salts.

Cobalt is an element which is required by intestinal micro-organisms for the synthesis of vitamin B 12, and for enzyme action in the body. Deficiency in this mineral results in emaciation and listlessness.

Iodine, a mineral element, appears to be a constituent of the hormone thyroxine which is produced by the thyroid gland. The thyroid gland, through its production of the hormone, regulates the basal metabolic rate and the functions of growth, reproduction and lactation. A deficiency

161

in iodine is indicated by an enlargement of the thyroid gland in the neck. Reproductive failure is also attributed to a deficiency of iodine. The iodine content in herbiage depends upon the amount of iodine in the soil, and, therefore, wide variations can occur. Traces of iodine occur in most foods.

Manganese is important in the animal body as an enzyme catalyst or activator. Symptoms of manganese deficiency in laboratory animals were slow growth, defective bone structure, and reproductive failures. Most green foods and rice bran are adequate sources of manganese.

Zinc has been found to be a component of every tissue in the animal body. Zinc plays an important role in enzymatic reactions. Deficiency in zinc is manifested by subnormal growth and depressed appetite. A good source of zinc is in the bran and germ of cereal grains.

Molybdenum is associated with copper in the animal body. Its role is in enzyme action. Deficiency symptoms have not been reported under normal conditions.

Selenium is regarded as an important mineral element in animal nutrition because of its toxicity. The symptoms include dullness, stiffness of the joints, lameness and hoof deformities. The toxic effects of selenium are reduced when high protein foods are administered to animals.

The nutritional requirements of other mineral elements have not been determined to any practical significance. Most of the mineral needs are said to be involved in chemical reactions in the animal body. Their exact functional roles have not been ascertained.

Vitamins

Vitamins are organic substances necessary in the diet in very small amounts. They functi.. as cellular catalysts in conjunction with bodily enzymes. This means that vitamins cause or accelerate a necessary chemical change in the metabolism of the body without their being permanently affected by the reaction. When animals were maintained on a chemically balanced diet containing only purified proteins, carbohydrates, fats and necessary minerals, it was not possible to sustain their life. Additional factors that are present in natural foods were required, and those factors were vitamins! Therefore, from the standpoint of the intermediary metabolism of the brain, nerve and other bodily cells, an adequate supply of essential vitamins is of great importance. Experimental and clinical studies provide practical evidence that defective bodily function at the enzymatic level, in which vitamins play an important role, may seriously affect physiological and behavioral functions of the animal. Unfortunately, the vitamin needs for elephants must be extrapolated from the known requirements for domestic beef cattle and horses.

Vitamin A is essential to promote normal growth and development of bones and teeth, to maintain the integrity of epithelial tissue, and to trigger the chemical reaction necessary for night vision. A deficiency in vitamin A impedes normal growth and development of bones and teeth and causes normal secretory epithelium to be replaced by a dry, keratinized epithelium which is more susceptible to invasion by infectious organisms. Inadequate supply of vitamin A can also cause night blindness. Vitamin A is not obtainable in the natural state. It is derived from carotene which is found in fresh green fodder, and good quality hays. The liver transforms the carotene to vitamin A. Unfortunately, carotene is unstable in the presence of oxygen and light, and it deteriorates with storage. Hays that are a year or more in storage may not contain sufficient carotene to convert to an adequate amount of vitamin A when ingested by elephants. All pigmented (particularly yellow) vegetables and fruits such as sweet potatoes, carrots, pumpkins, papayas, tomatoes, apricots and peaches are a good source of carotene and easily converted to vitamin A. Another good source of vitamin A is cod liver oil, and of course, vitamin A can be obtained in synthetic form in animal food stores.

Animal nutritionists claim that a dietary source of a group of vitamins known as B-complex (Bl, B2, B3, B6, and

B12) and the vitamins C and K is not considered necessary, because the B-complex and vitamin K are synthesized in the required amounts by the intestinal micro-organisms, and vitamin C is synthesized in the tissue of animals. However, this normal process of vitamin synthesis can be impaired by starvation, shortage of protein, cobalt deficiency or excessive levels of antibiotics or other medications. Sunlight is essential to the synthesis of vitamin C in the tissue, so elephants kept indoors for long periods of time without exposure to the sunlight may not be able to manufacture their own vitamin C.

Symptoms of B-complex vitamin deficiency includes loss of appetite, fatigueability, increased aggressiveness, lesions on the pink parts of the mouth and eyes, bilateral skin disorders, diarrhea, loss of weight and cessation of growth. Scurvy may result from deficiency of vitamin C which is marked by a lack of strength, restlessness, ulcerated gums, fetid breath and tissue hemorrhages. Deficiency in vitamin K results in uncontrollable hemorrhages.

If deficiencies in vitamin B-complex, C and K are suspected, they may be supplied by synthetic dietary supplements which are available commercially in animal feed stores.

Vitamin D is essential for the absorption of calcium and phosphorus from the food in the intestines. This vitamin is usually obtained from sun cured hay and exposure to sunlight. Elephants confined indoors for long periods of time without exposure to sunlight may develop a vitamin D deficiency resulting from a failure to extract and utilize calcium adequately and consequently may result in tetany. Calcium is essential for elephants to cope with the stresses they encounter in transportation, loading and unloading from vehicles, and during circus acts. Insufficient calcium reserves under these conditions may also result in tetany. Deficiency in vitamin D may be restored by dietary supplements.

Vitamin E is essential for normal fertility in animals. Its availability in the diet is related to the presence of adequate amounts of selenium. Low quality hay unsupplemented with grain may cause a deficiency in this vitamin. The lack of adequate amounts of vitamin E may be one of the major factors in the unsuccessful reproduction of elephants in captivity. Hay grown in high selenium earth ordinarily provides adequate amounts of vitamin E. Dietary supplements often contain appropriate amounts of this vitamin.

The important thing to remember about vitamins is that they are required in relatively small amounts in the body in order to effect their catalytic action. Excessive amounts of oil soluble vitamins (A, D, E, and K) are toxic! Vitamin D toxicity, for example, is symptomatic in animals by bone abnormalities, calcified deposits in blood vessels, heart and other soft tissues, loss of body weight, and general weakness. Therefore, caution should be observed in supplementing vitamins of A, D, E, and K.

Parlsey is an herb which is customarily used to garnish or season human food, but most people push it aside because of its slightly bitter taste. However, it is little known that parsley is highly nutritious. It contains a lot of protein, iron, calcium, phosphorus, potassium and vitamins A, B1, B2, B3, and C. It is relatively inexpensive. This fresh, green herb might be a relatively safe dietary supplement for elephants. Animals are known to be aware of their dietary deficiencies and they will select foods which will provide the necessary nutrients. Therefore, if elephants eat the parsley they will be supplementing their deficiency, and if they refuse the parsley, it will suggest an adequate amount of these nutrients. A simple experimental offer of parsley to a herd of circus elephants revealed them eating the green fresh herb voraciously.

Symptoms of nutritional deficiency in elephants are difficult to detect because during the usual body chemical reactions, various necessary ingredients such as minerals, etc., are cannibalized from tissues and organs containing them. It is only when these important ingredients for body chemistry are exhausted that symptoms began to appear. In elephants, because of their huge body size, this may take a lot of time. When symptoms of malnutrition appear, serious damage to vital organs and the nervous systems may already have occurred. Therefore, preventive maintenance nutrition is urged by supplementing the usual hay and grain diet of elephants with naturally green leafy vegetables, fruits, nuts and vitamins and minerals.

Recipe for Baby Elephant Diet

Under normal conditions in the wild state, a baby elephant suckles from its mother's teats shortly after it is born, and weaning does not occur until around two years of age. The survival rate of baby elephants born in captivity has not been very impressive. Abandonment and rejection of the baby elephant by the mother is one of the major reasons, especially in the case of a first pregnancy. Therefore, a nourishing formula should be available in case the feeding of a newborn elephant becomes the responsibility of the trainer or handler.

The following formula has been successfuly used in the feeding of a number of Asian and African baby elephants by elephant trainer "Smokey"Jones and others.

1 ¾ gals. water
3 tablespoons salt
4 cups rice
½ teaspoon D-Ca-Fos
3 cups minute oatmeal
2 cups wheatgerm
2 cups dark Karo syrup
1 lb. peanut butter
8 oz. honey
12 ½ oz. applesauce or other fruit
1 megavitamin and multi-mineral capsule

In a 3-gallon container, boil 1 3/4 gallons of water. Add the salt and the 4 cups of rice. Simmer for about 1/2 hour, then cover the container with a lid and let mixture come to a boil. Reduce heat and simmer until the rice is soft. Then add 3 cups of oatmeal and stir while contents simmer until oatmeal is cooked. Turn off the heat and add the remaining ingredients while stirring so that the ingredients are mixed well.

The prepared formula should have a liquid consistency. More water may be added to the mixture to achieve this. A 1/2 gallon plastic calf nursing bottle is filled 1/2 full with the formula, then the correct amount of calf "milk replacer" (the amount is determined by weight on the label) is added and sufficient water to fill the bottle. The ingredients are shaked well before feeding. The formula is served warm, NOT HOT!

The baby elephant trunk is raised and held against the head above the eyes while lifting the head at the same time. The nipple is placed in the elephant's mouth and the baby is allowed to suckle. It is important that the person doing the feeding is situated in a fixed position and not to move with the elephant if it should decide to move away from the nippled bottle. The infant elephant must learn that it must stand still in order to be fed. Baby elephants have a tendency to move around a lot while suckling, if allowed to do so, and therefore the person holding the bottle will be moving about a lot and this becomes tiring. When full, the baby elephant will back away from the hand-held bottle.

The formula is fed every four hours around the clock. The baby elephant is permitted to eat as much as it desires. A new batch of formula should be in the process of preparation while the previous one is being consumed by the baby elephant.

CHAPTER 16

ELEPHANT TRAINING

Most of the elephants in captivity in America and other parts of the world have been captured in the National Parks of Africa and Asia. Elephants captured in the wild and selected for export are usually about 1-2 year old females. Male elephants are less desireable because of their unpredictable behavior at maturity. Asian elephants have been preferred for circus acts because of their docility. African elephants are said to be more difficult to train. The technique of capturing baby African elephants in the wild was reported by the author in the May 1973 issue of *Zoonooz*, a publication of the San Diego Zoo. The article describes the capturing of the seven female African elephants now at the San Diego Wild Animal Park, while they were in the Wankie National Park in Rhodesia.

The exact date when man first achieved the superior mentality and ability to capture and to train elephants to perform various activities on command is lost in antiquity. The earliest and most famous historical account of trained elephants was in Hannibal's military campaign about 277 B. C. Obviously, elephant training was practiced for some time before that date.

Man has been associated with trained elephants in captivity for approximately 3000 years, but the complete methods of training elephants have never appeared in print. The methods of training elephants are usually perpetuated by word of mouth from one African elephant trainer to another. And the Asian elephant trainers known as mahouts and oozies pass on their knowledge and skills from father to son for generations. Detailed elephant training techniques have been the most ardently kept secrets in the history of animal training. One can easily find books on dog and horse training, but not on elephant training. Prior to this book, only two publications have appeared which could be considered as sources of information relative to the care and management of elephants in captivity. One of these was A. J. W. Milroy entitled, *"A Short Treatise on the Management of Elephants"* (1922). The other one was by A. J. Ferrier, entitled *"The Care and Management of Elephants in Burma"* (1947). The authors dealt with general Asian elephant husbandry, but nothing of substance of training methods.

There are no schools in existence for the teaching of elephant training. The only source of information on elephant training is the wisdom of such living elephant circus trainers as: Robert "Smokey" Jones, Mac MacDonald, Bucky Steele, Rex Williams, and Barbara and "Buckles" Woodcock. These people have acquired their knowledge of elephant training from other great elephant trainers such as: Louis Reed, George Denham, Tony Smaha, Walter McLain, Joe Metcalf, Hugo Schmidt, Colonel Woodcock, "Cheerful" Gardner and others (all of whom are deceased,) plus many years of their own trial-and-error experience. The author is very grateful to the contemporary generous and concerned persons for their willingness to discuss the problems inherent in the care, management and training of elephants in captivity. At the present time, the only way anyone can obtain knowledge and experience in training elephants is through an apprenticeship as a "Bull Hand" in a circus with elephants. There is some instruction in the care and management of elephants by Wally Ross, at the Moorpark College, Institute of Wild and Exotic Animal Studies, Moorpark, California.

Elephants in most American and European zoos suffer unrelieved boredom. They are usually locked up in relatively small quarters that are easy to keep clean and make the beasts readily visible to the public. These generally sociable animals are usually found just standing, or if they are close enough to the public, they usually extend their trunk for a handout of peanuts or other morsels of food.

Observations have revealed that because of the lack of activity on the part of elephants, human visitors to the zoos spend comparatively little time at the elephant exhibits, whereas people attending circuses enjoy observing the elephants in the "picket line" that they had seen during the elephant act. Zoo elephants should be trained to perform some routine act regularly. With proper advertisement, elephant acts would draw the public to the zoos and the attendance would improve the zoo's economics from the added revenue. The Basle, Switzerland Zoo and the San Diego Wild Animal Park have elephant acts that are well attended. Changing the repertoire of the elephants from time to time would bring back spectators to the zoo.

In addition to the increased revenue to the zoo, captive elephants of both species would be physically and psychologically healthier if they were trained to perform some acts similar to those done by circus elephants. Before this can be achieved, the attitudes of zoo directors and funding agencies will have to be changed relative to elephants and their exhibition. Personnel will have to be trained to be more than just animal keepers whose responsibilities are usually to keep the quarters clean and to feed and water the elephants. This means that the current salaries will have to be raised considerably in order to attract personnel with elephant training experience. The increased salary and improved status of present elephant caretakers should motivate them to seek additional education and experience in elephant training.

In changing from simply exhibiting elephants to performing elephants in zoos, public safety should be given high priority. The viewing public should be physically protected from the potential danger that is always present due to the massive strength, size and weight of elephants.

170

Once having established a safe arena, the sagacity and agility of these magnificent and fascinating animals will enthrall the viewing public.

Zoos with elephants should also set up an elephant training school. The zoos usually have fairly adequate facilities for the care and maintenance of elephants. The major problem is the lack of young personnel with elephant training experience. There are currently a number of older and retired persons thoughout the country with many years of elephant training experience. These persons could be persuaded to take over the leadership of such elephant training schools, if they were offered the proper incentives. Fees could be charged for such training and the revenue would help pay staff salaries.

Fortunately, this author was successful in persuading Robert "Smokey" Jones, an elephant trainer of some 35 years of experience, to describe and demonstrate his techniques of training elephants in captivity. Most of what follows in this chapter is what Smokey narrated to this author, and his demonstrations are illustrated by the accompanying photographs of his elephant named "Tika."

The ideal age at which elephants should be trained is between three and five years. At that age, the elephant is old enough to eat solid food of sufficient variety to assure adequate nourishment for growth and the maintenance of optimum health and strength. Also, at this age, the elephant's muscles are sufficiently developed so that it can physically endure the strenuous muscle activity during training. In addition, the elephant has not yet learned a maladaptive lifestyle, and that is important in establishing a working relationship between the trainer and the elephant.

When the young elephant is first accepted for training, it should undergo a thorough physical examination. The elephant should be walked briskly by an assistant and the trainer should observe the animal's gait. Examination of the walking elephant should be done from the right and left sides, from the rear, and while the elephant is walking toward the trainer. The elephant should display adequate balance and coordination while walking. At a brisk pace of walking the young elephant should freely swing its head and trunk from side to side. Any impairment of movement, limping, crippling or favoring should be noted and the cause ascertained. Muscle disorders and skeletal deformities will seriously impede the elephant's training.

The feet should be thoroughly examined for cracking of the toe nails, hang nails, infections, foreign bodies in the sole pads, etc. All abnormal conditions should be appropriately treated and cured prior to training.

The body should be examined for cuts, bruises, sores, infections, lice infestations and appropriately treated.

The elephant's effort at defecation and urination should be observed for difficulty and irritation. The fecal boli should be examined for unusually strong odor, consistency, quantity, color, and the presence of worms. A urine sample should be taken and examined for odor, color, clearness, and a test for sugar content.

The elephant's eyes should be examined. The trainer should pass his hand to each eye to check for the blinking reflex. This is one method for checking for blindness. The eye and the surrounding conjunctival tissue should be examined for infections, injuries, and inflammation.

The elephant's mouth should also be examined. The tongue should be a clear pinkish color. The teeth should be checked for growth and alignment. The inside of the mouth should be examined for sores, injury and infections. The area around the mouth should be examined for cracking of the skin especially at the corners, and for other bruises, cuts and infections.

The young elephant should receive proper nourishment in order to maintain its health and strength during training. The young elephant up for training should be observed during its feeding habit. A good appetite will indicate a healthy elephant. Only small amounts of hay should be given at any time, but as frequently as the elephant will eat it. Large amounts of hay should not be given at one time as much of it will be soiled with urine and excrement, and tossed by the elephant onto its back and around the surrounding area and thus wasted. However, a surplus of hay can be provided during the last feeding in the evening, so that some of it will absorb the urine and thus help to keep the area under the elephant relatively dry, and the surplus hay will make the elephant more comfortable and warm when it lies down to sleep.

Initial Elephant Training Maneuvers

The initial training maneuver is to teach the elephant to raise each foot individually on command. After the elephant has learned this behavior, it will make subsequent training maneuvers much easier not only on the elephant but the trainer as well.

To get the elephant to raise its hind leg backward, as seen in Figure 40, the trainer places the bull hook low down on the front part of the hind foot just above the toe nails. With repeated stimulation of the area with the bull hook, the trainer says "foot," as the elephant moves its foot away from the irritating points of the bull hook. When the leg is elevated to the desired height, the trainer says "steady." After the elephant has maintained the leg in the elevated position for an adequate length of time, the trainer says "all right," and the elephant is allowed to place its foot back down on the ground. This procedure is repeated until the elephant voluntarily raises its designated leg upon command without the use of the bull hook.

To train the elephant to raise its front foot forward as seen in Figure 41, the bull hook is placed at the back of the front foot and pulled forward as the trainer says "foot." When the elephant raises its leg to the desired height by repeated use of the bull hook, the trainer says "steady," and the elephant must keep its leg elevated until the trainer says "all right" at which time the elephant is allowed to place its foot back on the ground.

These procedures are repeated many times until the elephant will raise any foot indicated by a touch from the bull

173

174

Fig. 41 Elephant taught to raise foreleg on command.

hook and on verbal command. The selection of the leg to be raised should be done randomly, instead of in a regular sequence. Otherwise, the elephant may raise the leg it learned in sequence instead of the leg that is selected for elevation.

Training an Elephant to Lie Down

Training an elephant to lie down has many benefits. It is the preferred position of the elephant when the back or the underside of the elephant must be cleaned, examined or treated. It is most essential to be able to have the elephant lie down on a preferred side when surgery is contemplated, or an anaesthetic is to be administered. If the elephant is anesthetized while standing, it may be injured when it falls, or it may land in an inappropriate position for a desired treatment or surgery. An elephant in a lying down posture is also a protective measure for the trainer or other personnel, just in case it should resist treatment and attempt to attack or escape. And finally, it is from the lying down position that other elephant training maneuvers are started.

Training an elephant to lie down is usually done on a grassy area or on the bare soft ground, and not on a concrete or other hard surface.

Lying down is a natural position for the elephant, so it is not difficult for the animal to assume this posture. Nonetheless, it apparently is not a very comfortable position for mature elephants because they do not remain in a down position very long either in the wild or in captivity. However, training is necessary to get the elephant to lie down on command, and thus the following procedure must be observed.

The initial procedure for training an elephant to lie down on command is to drive a steel stake into the ground about 10 feet in front of the elephant and another stake about 10 feet behind the elephant. One end of a chain or rope, of about 20 feet in length, is tied around one front foot and the other end is fastened to the stake in front of the elephant. Another

176

chain or rope, of the same length, is tied around one hind foot and secured to the stake in back of the elephant. Then both of the front legs and the hind legs are tied together in a figure eight fashion as indicated in Figure 42.

A length of rope is tied around the elephant's neck as indicated in Figure 43. It is tied snuggly but not too tight, so that the rope can be moved about the neck.

Then a long rope is tied around a hind leg on the side to which the elephant will be brought to lie down. That is, if the elephant will be brought to lie down on the left side, the rope will be tied around the rear left leg, and if the elephant is to be brought down on the right side, then the rope will be tied around the right rear leg. The other end of the long rope is then passed under the elephant, then under the loop of rope around the elephant's neck, and over the elephant's back and to the same side as the leg to which the rope was tied, as indicated in Figure 44. The loose end of this rope will be used to pull down the elephant to the ground on its side as indicated in Figure 45.

When the elephant is on its side, a steel stake is driven into the ground about 10 feet away from the back of the elephant, and the loose end of the pull-down rope is tied in a bolan knot (to put over the stake easily and to remove easily) to the stake in order to hold the elephant down on its side as shown in Figure 46.

When the elephant is on its side and tied to the stake, the trainer while standing close to the elephant's head says "steady" to the elephant and he simultaneously touches the top of the elephant's head with his hand or a bull hook, until the elephant lies motionless on its side, as shown in the above figure. Sometimes some negative reinforcement may be required to keep the elephant from resisting to obey commands.

After the elephant has become accustomed to lying on its side, the rope holding the elephant down is untied from the stake. Then the trainer says "all right" and the elephant will usually attempt to stand up. A few upward stimulations with the bull hook on the underside of the elephant will encourage the elephant to get up. If the elephant cannot stand up, it is probably because the legs were tied too close together. Therefore, the ropes tied in figure eight around the elephant's legs will have to be loosened but not untied after the elephant stands up on command, it is allowed to remain standing for a short while, giving it an opportunity to recover from this experience. This procedure is repeated until the elephant lies down on its side and stands up without force, and on command. For a three year old elephant, this procedure may have to be repeated 50 or more times, whereas for an adult elephant, this procedure may have to be repeated fewer times.

Procedure for Training an Elephant to Sit-Up

An elephant in a sitting position is a spectacular spectacle, partly because of the enormous size of the elephant and partly because wild elephants are rarely seen in this unnatural posture. An elephant in a sitting position is frequently seen in circus acts.

The procedure for training an elephant to sit up starts with the lying-down position. Therefore, the elephant must be taught to lie down on command. (See above procedure for training elephant to lie down.) When the elephant lies down on command, then the rope tied in a figure eight around the front feet is untied, but the rope around the hind feet remains tied in place. The rope from the front leg to the stake in the ground remains tied as indicated in Figure 47.

While the elephant is down on its side as shown in the above figure, the rope that holds the elephant down is loosened and the trainer says "all right" to the elephant, and as the elephant proceeds to stand up, it assumes a posture of being on its front leg elbows, a half-way-up position, then the pull-down rope is tightened again by an assistant, and the trainer says "steady" as indicated in Figure 48. The elephant is pulled back down and allowed to assume this half-way-up posture several times until it remains in the half-way-up position on command.

Fig. 42   *Elephant legs tied together in a figure-eight knot.*

179

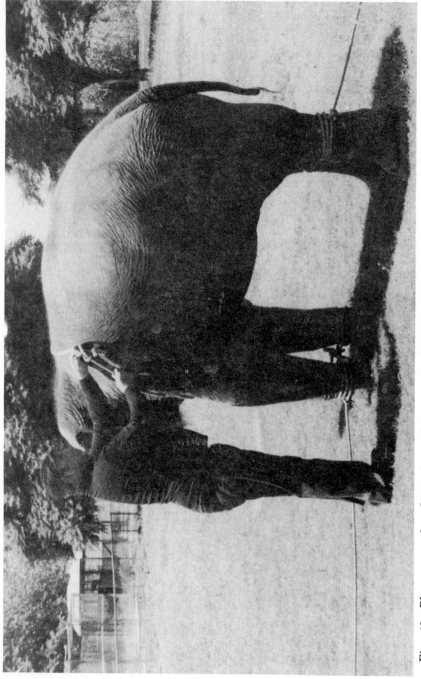

Fig. 43 Placement of a short piece of rope around the elephant's neck.

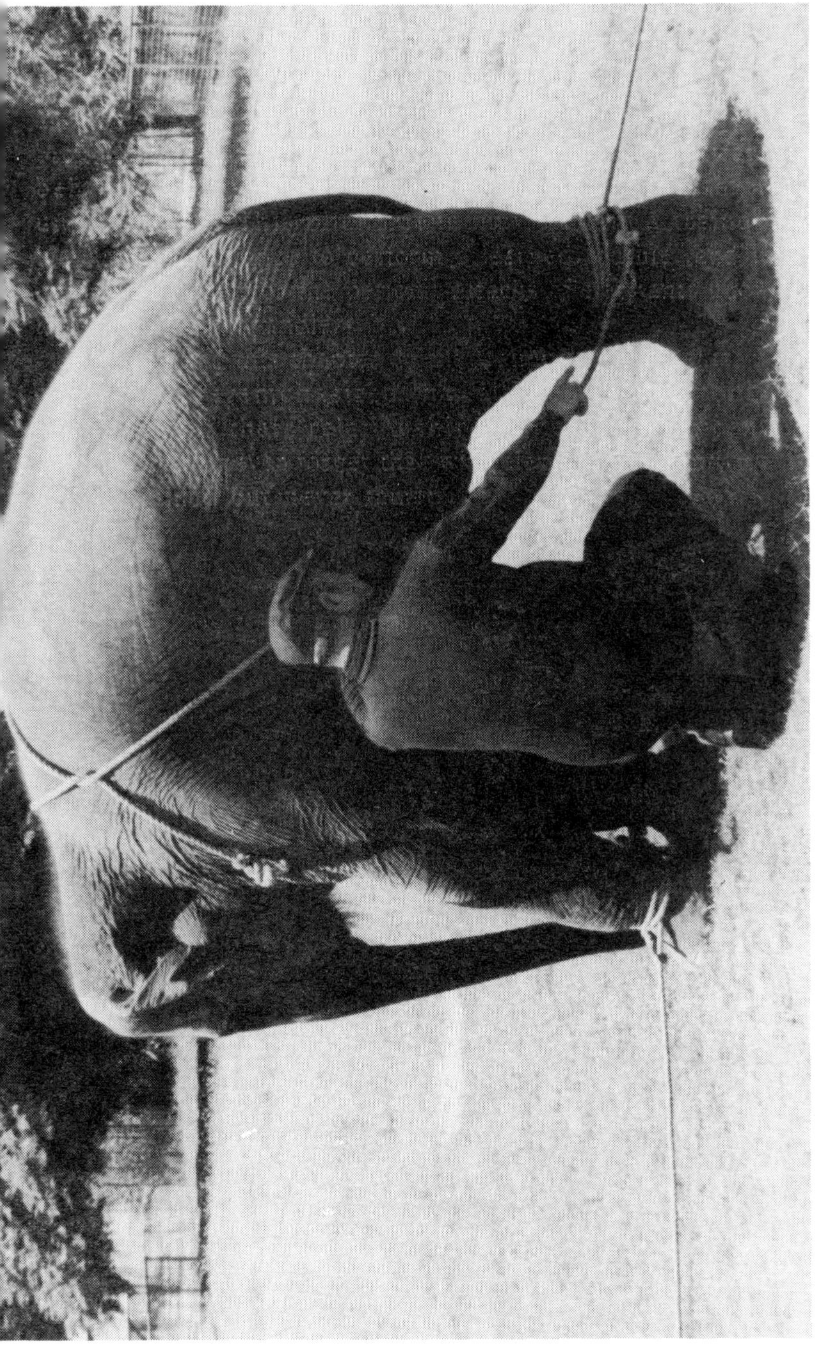

Fig. 44 Attachment of the pull-down rope.

Fig. 45   *Position of rope and trainers ready to pull elephant down on its side.*

Fig. 46   Elephant on its side after pull-down and placement of steel stake 10 feet from its back.

183

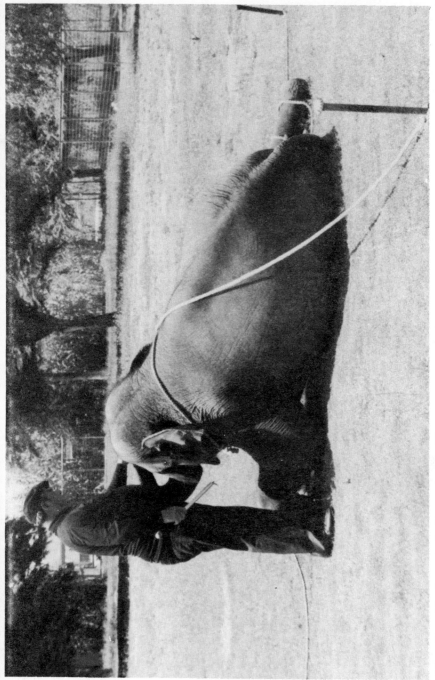

Fig. 47   Elephant in half-way-up position.

184

Fig. 48   Rope around right hind foot and attached to 4th stake driven 10 feet from elephant's feet and opposite to 3rd stake at back of elephant.

At this time, a fourth steel stake is driven into the ground about 10 feet from the feet of the elephant, in a position directly opposite to the stake on the other side of the elephant to which the hold-down rope is tied. Another rope is tied around the right hind foot of the elephant with the knot in front. The other end of this rope is tied to the fourth stake with enough tension to prevent the elephant from putting its right hind leg under its body as it starts to get up, as indicated in Figure 49. The rope tied to the stake in and around the front legs of the elephant is then untied from the stake, but the other end remains tied to the elephant's front foot as shown in the above figure. The rope binding the elephant's rear feet together is now removed. The elephant's trunk is then grasped with the trainer's left hand and held against the elephant's forehead as is also shown in the above Figure 49. At this time all the ropes tied to stakes are unfastened except the rope holding the right hind leg from going under the elephant. The elephant will thus assume the position as indicated in Figure 50, with two assistants holding the ropes tied to the front feet.

The next step is where the early training of the elephant to raise its foot on command pays off. The elephant is commanded to raise both of its front feet by the trainer saying "foot" and the assistants pulling the front legs up with the ropes simultaneously with the command. The elephant's right foot is then placed on the trainer's left thigh as shown in Figure 50. The trainer then says, "sit" to the elephant, while stimulating the right foot with the bull hook, and the assistant helps the elephant to raise its left foot with the attached rope. The elephant's trunk is raised further up on the elephant's forehead, and the trainer pushes the elephant back to transfer the weight to the elephant's rump and away from the trainer's thigh. This is the first time the elephant is in an unnatural position and it must learn how to balance itself while in a sitting position. The trainer can assist the elephant in learning how to balance itself in the sitting position by firmly controlling the elephant's trunk. Both front feet are stimulated by the bull hook so that the legs are raised high and the elephant assumes the sitting position. When this position is accomplished by the elephant, the trainer says "all right" and the elephant is allowed to fall back to the ground on its front feet. The elephant should not be allowed to sit in this posture very long on the first few trials. The above procedure is repeated until the elephant assumes the sitting position satisfactorily on command without the trainer's assistance, as shown on Figure 51. With each trial, the elephant is commanded to "sit" a longer time.

Procedure in Training an Elephant to Sit on a Tub

The first step in the procedure of training a young elephant to sit on a tub is to drive two steel stakes into the ground about 10 feet apart. Then, ropes about 15 feet long are tied to each of the elephant's hind feet, and the opposite ends of the ropes are tied to the stakes.

The elephant is then command to "back up," while the trainer holds the elephant's trunk up against its forehead and he pushes the animal backward until the leg ropes are tight. This part of the procedure should be repeated many times so that the elephant will learn to walk backwards in a straight line. The elephant is commanded to come forward by saying "move up" while pulling the trunk away from the forehead.

When the elephant has learned to back up in a straight line, a tub is placed behind the elephant by an assistant as is indicated in Figure 52. Then the elephant is gently tapped on the chin with the bull hook, and the trunk is raised high against the elephant's forehead while pushing the animal back and simultaneously commanding "back up." Since the elephant cannot back up farther than the length of the ropes that are tied around the hind legs and fastened to the stakes, the elephant begins to squat down as it continues to be urged backward and it finally sits down on the tub as indicated in Figure 53.

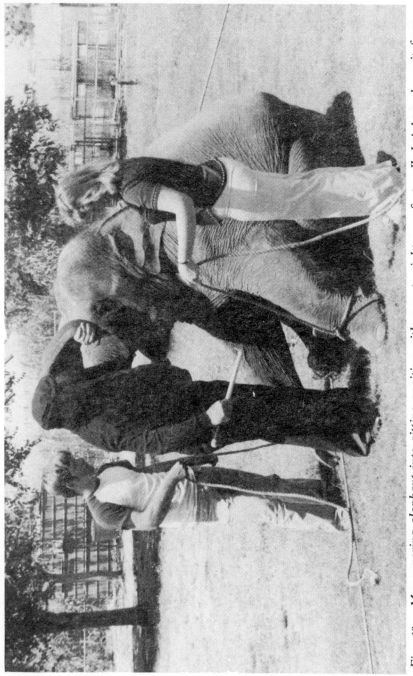

Fig. 49   Maneuvering elephant into sitting position with rope to right rear foot pulled tight to keep it from going under the elephant as it assumes a sitting position.

Fig. 50   While in a sitting position, elephant's right foot on trainer's left thigh.

189

Fig. 51 Elephant in sitting position with forefoot on kick without assistant.

Fig. 52   *Trunk against head, training elephant to back up to the length of ropes on hind legs, and   position of tub.*

191

Fig. 53   Elephant sitting on tub on command.

192

After the elephant is seated on the tub, the trainer commands the elephant to raise its front feet while he stimulates them with the bull hook. When the elephant raises its front feet to the required height while sitting on the tub, and balancing itself in that position, the trainer says "steady" as shown in Figure 54. The elephant should not be forced to stay in the tub sitting position very long during the first few trials. As soon as the elephant assumes the sitting position on the tub with its front feet up high, the trainer says "all right," and the elephant should be allowed to drop back down to the ground and to stand up from the sitting position. This procedure is repeated many times until the elephant learns to associate the commands with the related sitting position. When this stage of the training is accomplished, the ropes that were tied to the hind feet are removed and the routine is repeated until perfected.

Procedure to Train an Elephant to Stand Up on its Hind Legs

To train an elephant to stand up on its hind legs, it is necessary to command the elephant to "back up" into an inside corner of a building, against a strong wall, or a stack of bales of hay. Then the elephant is commanded to "foot" while it is being touched with the bull hook to both front feet. When the elephant goes up, it leans against the wall or hay stack for support and balances as indicated in Figure 55. This is a very unnatural position for the elephant to assume; therefore, the elephant should not be forced to remain in this posture very long during the first few trials. The elephant may become ruptured when forced to stand in this position too long during the early training period. As soon as the elephant stands up on its hind feet, it should be immediately allowed to come back down upon the ground at the command of "all right." After numerous trials the elephant's abdominal muscles will be strengthened to the point where support to the back will not be necessary. The elephant can then be commanded to assume this position anywhere.

The procedures described herein are recommended to be taught in the sequence in which they have been presented. These procedures will have to be repeated many, many, many times. This is where the virtue of patience described in an earlier chapter will be required.

If an elephant can learn a certain behavior or trick in a relatively few trials or in a relatively short time, it can be assumed that the elephant is prepared to behave in that manner. The trainer should realize that some elephants are more prepared to do certain behaviors and others are not. It does not mean that both kinds of elephants—prepared and unprepared—cannot be trained, but it will take more time to train the unprepared ones. In expanding the repertoire of trained behaviors of elephants, it should be more rewarding and satisfying in concentrating on those behaviors that elephants are prepared to perform, that is, easy for them to do.

Having trained an elephant to perform a variety of tricks, frequent rehearsals will be required so that the elephant will attain proficiency and excellence in the repertoire of its learned behaviors. The elephant is reputed to have a good memory, but the elephant trainer must always remember that all animals, including elephants, are subject to a phenomena which behavioral scientists refer to as "instinctual drift." This means that even though elephants are trained to behave in certain ways, they will tend to revert back toward instinctual behaviors regardless of reward or punishment. The explanation for this interference to learned behavior is that innate or instinctual behaviors are related to the basic neurological mechanisms with which animals are born, rather than to some principles of learning. Therefore, elephants will have to be rehearsed frequently in their learned behaviors in order to prevent the occurrence of instinctual drift.

In addition, elephant trainers will need to be aware that elephants, as well as other animals, have "wired-in" defense reactions which provide them with the capability to survive in their wild natural habitats. Their basic

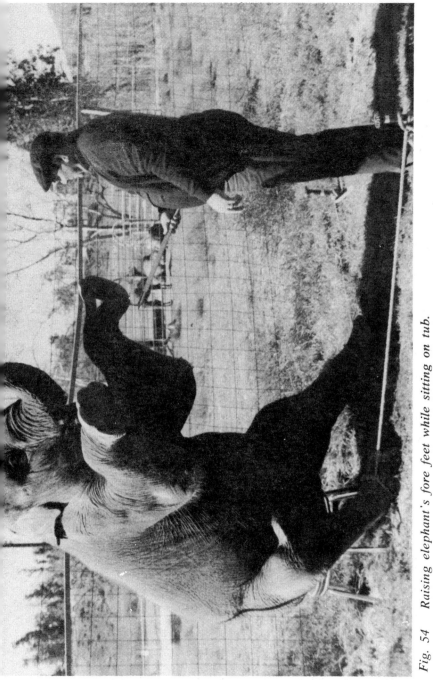

Fig. 54   *Raising elephant's fore feet while sitting on tub.*

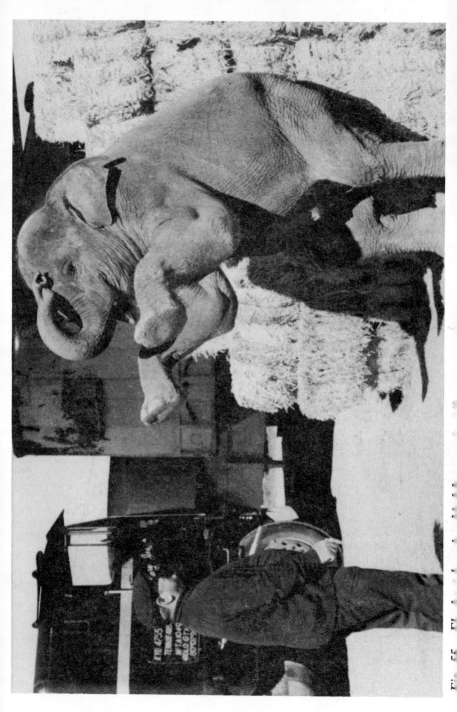

Fig. 55. El... ... ...

196

neurological equipment such as sensory receptors and motor apparatus prepares the animals to deal with situations that are found in their natural habitats. When elephants are brought into captivity, they may occasionally demonstrate behaviors which may seem inappropriate, skiddish or unreasonable. This phenomena may explain a trained elephant's reluctance to perform a learned routine, and it may also account for the periodic attacks of elephants upon their trainers or handlers.

In concluding this chapter on the training of elephants, it cannot be overemphasized that all elephant persons, regardless of their relationship to these magnificent animals, must never forget that wild elephants in captivity can be trained but never tamed!

CHAPTER 17

EPILOGUE

This book has tried to describe elephants as unique animals worthy of our interest and consideration. There are many different kinds of antelopes, horses, deer, and birds, but elephants are special. They are the largest land mammals on earth. In spite of their enormous weight and huge size, elephants are majestic, agile, formidable but usually tranquil creatures.

Elephants have been symbols of eloquence, splendor, esteem, dignity, strength and integrity. They have played a very important role in the evolution of human culture, economy and religion. Elephants are intelligent social creatures who demonstrate many human characteristics.

Ironically, their future existence is in jeopardy. The best estimate is that there are less than a million elephants in Africa, and approximately 30,000 of the Asian species, which are already endangered. There are only about 500 elephants, including both species, in captivity. These are held primarily in zoos and circuses around the world. The African species in the wild are rapidly dwindling. Many African countries, with native elephants, conduct regular cropping operations to reduce the population of elephants in their National Parks. Thousands of elephants are shot each year. Entire herds and family groups are wiped out. In case of drought, famine, fire, flooding, or some other natural disasters (like the drought in Kenya where thousands of elephants died,) the African elephant populations may be dangerously reduced.

If elephants are to exist at all, their survival will depend on how well they can be preserved in captivity. Unfortunately, not very much is known about elephant nutrition, diseases, care, management and training.

Ill-advisedly, the United States Government has restricted the importation of Asian elephants, and legislation is currently being considered to restrict the importation of African elephants. This action is wrong and unreasonable.

American environmentalists have managed to forestall the completion of a 100 million dollar dam project because to do so would endanger the existance of a three inch fish known as the snail darter. Similar pressure should be exerted on the legislators to prevent them from passing laws prohibiting the importation of elephants. Restricting the importation of elephants will increase the probability of their demise at a faster rate in their natural habitats.

Elephants should be imported and extensively studied so that we can learn the best way to protect them not only for their own welfare, but for the enjoyment of future generations of human beings. Studies of elephants in captivity are practically non-existent. Centers for the Study of Elephants should be established all over the world. Short-term and long-term research projects should be immediately undertaken while elephants are still available.

Zoologists, ethologists and animal psychologists should concentrate their research efforts on learning more about elephants in captivity. There is also room for scientists from other disciplines such as nutrition, veterinary medicine, etc. We don't know why elephants don't readily reproduce in captivity. We don't know why elephants are docile for years and suddenly turn on their keepers, sometimes causing serious injury or death. We don't know the function of the elephant's temporal glands, and the allegedly associated condition of musth. We don't have scientifically determined nutritional requirements for elephants. We have not ascertained the most efficient method of training elephants. These are the most pressing problems faced by people owning or caring for elephants. These problems could be solved in a reasonable length of time by adequate financing, well-directed research, and competent personnel. The Center for the Study of Elephants in Carson, California, is the first such organization dedicated to the scientific study of elephants in captivity. Some important research has already been published under its auspices. We hope someday to be able to explain and solve the problems related to elephants that have been described in this book. We are also dedicated to protect and perpetuate pachyderms!